LIVES OF MODERN WOMEN

General Editor: Emma Tennant

Rebecca West

Fay Weldon

VIKING

VIKING
Penguin Books Ltd, Harmondsworth, Middlesex, England
Viking Penguin Inc., 40 West 23rd Street, New York 10010, U.S.A.
Penguin Books Australia Ltd, Ringwood, Victoria, Australia
Penguin Books Canada Ltd, 2801 John Street, Markham, Ontario, Canada L3R 1B4
Penguin Books (N.Z.) Ltd, 182–190 Wairau Road, Auckland 10, New Zealand

First published 1985
Published simultaneously by Penguin Books

Made and printed in Great Britain by
Richard Clay (The Chaucer Press) Ltd,
Bungay, Suffolk
Set in Monophoto Photina

British Library Cataloguing in Publication Data

Weldon, Fay
   Rebecca West.—(Lives of modern women)
   1. West, rebecca—Biography   2. Authors,
   English—20th century—Biography
I. Title   II. Series
   823'.912   PR6045.E8Z/

ISBN 0–670–80627–7

Library of Congress Catalog Card Number: 85–51188

CONTENTS

LIST OF PLATES

1892	Born Cicily Isabel Fairfield in London. She was educated at George Watson's Ladies' College, Edinburgh.
1911	Joined the suffragist movement and the staff of the *Freewoman*.
1912	Became a political writer on the socialist newspaper the *Clarion*.
	Adopted the *nom de plume* Rebecca West, from a character in Ibsen's play *Rosmersholm*, in which she once acted.
1913	Met and began a love affair with H. G. Wells. It lasted some ten years.
1914	On 5 August their son Anthony was born.
1916	Her first book was published – a critical study of Henry James.
1918	Her first novel, *The Return of the Soldier*, was published. Between 1918 and 1966 she wrote many other novels.
1923	Lectured in the USA and formed a long-standing reviewing association with the *New York Herald Tribune*.

1930	Married Henry Maxwell Andrews, a banker. They lived together at their country house, Ibstone, in Buckinghamshire, with frequent visits to London and often travelling abroad.
1930s	Made several trips to the Balkans in the mid-thirties.
1941	Published *Black Lamb and Grey Falcon*, a much admired two-volume book on Yugoslavia. Superintended BBC wartime broadcasts to Yugoslavia.
1949	Attended the Nuremberg war crimes trials, and wrote her most famous work of non-fiction, *The Meaning of Treason*. Awarded the CBE.
1959	Created a Dame Commander, Order of the British Empire.
1968	Made a Companion of Literature. Henry Andrews died.
1983	Rebecca West died on 15 March at the age of ninety.

Rebecca West, that formidable elder stateswoman of English literature, died in 1983 at the age of ninety. Novelists do seem to live to ripe old ages. Perhaps they are nourished by the energy of their own inventiveness, or perhaps their pen and ink characters, so long as they're good enough, hang around like flesh and blood children to support them in their old age. It would be pleasant to think so. Tolstoy, Mauriac, Colette, Somerset Maugham, Graves, Priestley, West – but how, while they last, these Grand Old Men, Grand Old Women do loom over the younger generation of writers, making them feel mere literary upstarts, poseurs, by comparison with the Real Thing.

I met Rebecca West on occasion during her later years, and although I'm sure she never said anything which wasn't perfectly polite, she certainly frightened me – and not only by virtue of sheer seniority. Her reputation went ahead of her, and didn't help. Rightly or wrongly, she was said to have an all too caustic wit, a tendency to make searing personal comment, and to be given to publicly despising the works of younger writers. So I stayed, when possible, the other side of the room.

I knew her too through the books of her son, Anthony West: these did not make her seem an attractive person, but troubled, troublesome and false, a woman determined to damage her only child. And Anthony West's view of the world is not to be ignored – he himself being a writer of power, wit and intelligence, as his biography of his father (*H. G. Wells – Aspects of a Life*) was to prove. Too late, alas, to convince his mother of what he most wanted her to accept, and which she never wished to believe – that he, like his parents, was a writer of stature. The book was not published until after her death. Around such terrible acrimonies are some literary careers formed. I cannot believe they help.

I had, moreover, seen photographs of Rebecca West over the years, and preferred the evidence of the printed page to that of my own eyes, as it is tempting to do. In these black and white versions of her, she scarcely seems the kind of person one would start chatting to on top of a London bus or while delivering milk to her door, let alone at a literary party.

See her, magnificent, on her way to the Old Bailey, in 1960, to give evidence at the *Lady Chatterley's Lover* trial. How firm her jaw, how steady her eye! Argue with her? Remonstrate? You must be joking! Here is a woman who has seen a lot, thought a lot, and come to many unwelcome conclusions, all of them right. She has no time, we know, for dreary puritanism – so D. H. Lawrence and his book will be exonerated from suspicion of tending to deprave and corrupt. The opposition doesn't stand a chance: just a little Westian touch – the floodgates move and a torrent of sexual explicitness floods through, for good or bad.

A somehow un-intimate person, more at home at the hub of world affairs than chatting over the kitchen table: as if knowing more than ordinary mortals, she is not prepared to accept the properly female form of fictional invention, but must boldly venture out into the male world of journalism and political comment. What sort of woman is this, who won't grow old gracefully, silently?

Here she is in her middle age, receiving an Achievement Award Certificate from President Truman in the late 1940s, she having been one of the few women sent officially to attend the Nuremberg trials after World War Two. That was when the developed world (which in those days was thought to be the whole world) first came face to face with its own murderous nature. Out of this experience Rebecca West wrote one of her best-known books, *The Meaning of Treason*. And though I suspect she looked too myopically through patriotic glasses, and failed to grasp the hopefulness of what she saw – as concepts of loyalty and morality, for centuries poles apart, at last began to fuse – the very existence of the book, the sheer masculine force of the title, gave her a status usually accorded only to men – that of *knowing best*, of receiving awards from presidents. What to talk to her about? Best smile, nod, keep a distance.

And then of course there was that one great basic, awesome fact, that she was not just Miss West, Ms West, or Mrs Maxwell Andrews, she was *Dame Rebecca West*. In 1959 she had been made a Dame Commander of the British Empire. A Dame, by sheer force of intelligence. Trickier still.

So one way or another, fairly or unfairly, I suspected Rebecca West of being admired rather than loved. Indeed, of being admirable rather than lovable. But then, whoever said writers have to be *nice*? They don't. They just have to be good writers and niceness may even be a contra-indication of the state. Had she been a man she would instantly have been excused aggression, wilfulness, and parental absurdity. I have no doubt that she was a great deal less difficult a woman than, say, Tolstoy was a man: we continue (or many of us do) with the residual notion that women writers should be gentle, kind, helpful, reflective, reassuring. Feminine, in fact, in the traditional meaning of the word. 'Angels of the House', as Virginia Woolf put it. It is an absurd notion.

What Rebecca West was, and to my mind this excuses all personal error and all bad behaviour, was an extraordinary, marvellous – albeit rather ill-disciplined – writer of fiction; a woman born to her literary vocation, in love with the human race as she could not be with individuals, unerring in her fictional vision; a novelist of wonderful animation, courage and compassion, and with an ability to see the world through the eyes of even those whom she most disliked. (The person may dislike many, but the person as writer can afford to dislike none.) But most of all because, flickering in and out of the black and white printed pages, as if richly coloured gems were hidden there, offered casually as gifts to her reader, there for the treasuring, are a wealth of somehow thrown-away observations, brilliant little glimmers of insight, exquisite, which make the hairs at the back of the literate neck rise. 'Children are a remarkable race,' she murmurs, 'because they want so much to murder so many people, and murder so few. But they have a bad criminal record.' The mind considers, reels, continues . . .

Or

'What's the good of music,' he asked, 'if there's so much cancer in the world?' There came a voice out of the darkness, speaking so earnestly that it was shaken with tears. 'What's the harm in cancer, if there's all this music in the world?'

I am prepared to forgive anyone anything if they can write like this, and she can, and quite often, not always, does. May I recommend three books of hers to you, if you are not already acquainted with her writing? *The Return of the Soldier* (1918), *The Judge* (1922) and, to my mind, the greatest and the best, *The Fountain Overflows* (1956).

They do not, unlike most novels written today, make easy reading. The last two are, to modern tastes, wandering, idiosyncratic, wilful and unlikely, and the first is stuffed with sentiments not acceptable to modern liberal thinking. Rebecca West's distaste for poverty shines through *The Return of the Soldier* and her dislike and fear of the servant classes through *The Judge*; only in *The Fountain Overflows*, written in her maturity, does she appear truly rich and kind, and to have finally forgiven herself (and everyone else), for which the reader can only be grateful.

The trick with a Rebecca West novel is to approach it with caution and respect, knowing that you have time and attention to spare. Don't assume you can skip, skim, or read carelessly; you can't. She is to be read word by word; and then, if only you allow her, she will construct such a convincing edifice around you that the longest afternoon, the weariest train journey will pass as if by magic. She will have led you by a caring fictional hand into another world: and you will have spent a more animating and enlightening time in that land than in this. I know no writer better able to do it.

The Return of the Soldier was published when Rebecca West was twenty-five; of the three I offer you it is the shortest and the simplest: the story of a young hero who comes home from the war to his adoring wife, his perfect marriage – but with his memory lost. It transpires that in fact he loves not his delectable wife, but a woman who would appear unlovable – a lower-class woman, shabby, pitiful, genteel. The novel has a misty magic about it; the sadness of the past, of passion spent. And it has that peculiar quality that the first novels of gifted writers often have, of something extraordinary discovered and rather hastily offered: a jewel freshly mined and only cursorily polished, because of the sudden intimation in the writer's mind, and so in the reader's too, of so much so wonderful to come.

The Judge, written over the next three years, is a rambling tale which much irritated Rebecca West's lover, H. G. Wells. 'It just *grew*' was his complaint, but her pride. It mingles a hopeless romanticism with an uneasy realism; it is totally unconvincing: it is a perfectly splendid book in spite of itself. A contemporary editor, were it to land on a publisher's desk today, would slash it to bits and deprive it of the power of its own idiosyncrasy. A young girl, an office junior in Edinburgh (a portrait of herself when young, they say, though I doubt it: the only resemblance seems to be that both Ellen

Melville and Rebecca West – or Cicily Fairfield, as she was born – both distributed feminist leaflets in the Edinburgh streets), captures the fancy of Mr Yaverland from Essex, who at the beginning of the book seems to be in his late forties and by the end of it in his twenties. But it is Yaverland's mother, Marion, who is at the heart of the book: she has two sons, one horribly misbegotten, whom she despises (though he seems to do nothing despicable, except want his mother's love and not be particularly handsome), and the other conceived in love, whom she worships. This latter son is Ellen's lover. If there is a por- trayal of the author in the book, see it not in Ellen but in Marion; in the war with herself that Rebecca West fought in relation to her son Anthony: a dichotomy of love and hate, both unreasonable because both undeserved.

The Fountain Overflows, originally published in 1956, was reissued posthumously in 1984. Rebecca West worked on the book, off and on, for thirty years. It was the first part of an intended trilogy, of which the second part, *This Real Night*, was published for the first time in 1984. The final, though incomplete, part, *Cousin Rosamund*, is to be published in 1985. *The Fountain Overflows* concerns itself with the growing-up of a young girl in Edinburgh and is obliquely autobiographical – a description of a sensitive and talented child, Rose Aubrey, growing up in genteel, educated poverty. The mother in the book, Mrs Aubrey, struggles and suffers as Rebecca's mother, Mrs Fairfield, struggled and suffered. The father charms and abandons as Mr Fairfield in his time charmed and abandoned his wife and children. The two sisters are there, Letitia and Winifred Fairfield, portrayed as Cordelia and Mary Aubrey. But there is the addition, the sheer invention, of a younger brother, little Richard Quin, so charming, so fetching, so endearing in print, as to be, I think, one of the more powerful invented characters in all literature. (This is a large claim: but you will have to read the book to disagree with me.) To my mind, Richard Quin, with all his winning ways, lives forever. He is the little brother any family of girls should have had, even if they never did. The male principle, safely, endearingly confined in the child's body, full of affection and asexual intimacy, yet without the power to hurt and desert.

Try her other works by all means: *Black Lamb and Grey Falcon* (if you like Yugoslavia, that is – it is very *long*), *The Thinking Reed*, *The Birds Fall Down*, *The Harsh Voice* – all will give pleasure, but none as much, I think, as do these three. It would be a pity to try the lesser works, get bored, and give up.

I also, though more tentatively, recommend *The Young Rebecca*, a collection of Rebecca West's early journalistic essays and reviews. Written in the early years of the century by a very young woman, they remain both diverting and pertinent today – though you may think her airy dismissal of the likes of Strindberg disquieting. She is more charitable in her fiction; even in *The Return of the Soldier* she kindly remarks, 'There is, you know, really room for all of us: we each have our peculiar use' – and what can be more charitable than that! But the kindness is fitful, and reserved for fiction. She concludes, for instance, by remarking in her 1981 introduction to *The Meaning of Treason*, 'I cannot think that espionage can be recommended as a technique for building an impressive civilization. It's a lout's game.' Here we have it: the nub of my protest: the condemnation, not quite on moral grounds, not quite on class grounds, but managing both at once, as if they were the same. She is so ineffably *English*. 'A lout's game'. Now me, I feel sorry for louts. I see myself as potentially loutish. Rebecca West doesn't, isn't, couldn't be, is too much a lady. In this lies her power, her capacity to intimidate. I know myself as capable of treason as the next person, and bow my head in shame. She knew she would never do such a thing. Never!

Dame Rebecca West, having lived so long and so usefully, her books admired and read (by some with real pleasure, though no doubt by others out of a sense of literary duty), published and republished by dedicated and respectful publishers, now becomes the subject of that literary gossip which so delights those who can't wring sufficient satisfaction out of writers by simply reading their books. (I include myself in their number.) She had in her youth a long and hopeless love affair with H. G. Wells, in which, by their son's account, she was the one who loved most, and lost. And by Wells's own account, in that slice of autobiography *H. G. Wells in Love*, recently published, to have been well and soundly loved by him – in so far as he was capable of love, which seems in question. It is the ins and outs of this old love affair, the wheres and whyfores, the whens and hows, which so attract the attention of the reading public, and to which I now turn my attention. A long-gone love, in the end, being so much more powerful and compelling a notion than present literature, or any current merely sexual literary scandal. Wells and West! The encounter of giants –

Godzilla meets King Kong in the Writing World of Long Ago.

If this is an ignoble end, another nail in the coffin of any notion that literary personality and literary work can be kept apart, I am sorry. I have no shame, though, in what comes next, of having simply *made a lot up*, of having invented conversations, of being a fly on the seaside boarding-house wall – on the grounds that what is made up, invented, is often truer than what happens in reality; the latter, drifting, chaotic, without shape or form, and usually open to so many interpretations as to make non-sense of any attempt to understand or define from the outside what was actually going on in the inside. In fiction – in plays, novels, films – actions have clear purpose and proper meaning: people do this because they think or feel that. (Script editors insist upon it; so do audiences and readers.) In real life people act in the most part on impulse, and are only vaguely motivated, if at all. You can search all around for the 'because' and never find it. The character, nature and appearance of living people changes fitfully, from year to year, decade to decade. They insist on acting out of character. Better, if the biographer has a glimmer of the single thin consistent thread that runs through a life, to give up fact and take to fiction. It is as honourable a course as any.

FAY WELDON
FEBRUARY 1985

REBECCA WEST

REBECCA WEST

Your Delicious Bed

Letters from the Future to the Young Rebecca West

Dear Rebecca,

It is 4 August 1914. You are living in furnished lodgings in Hunstanton, Norfolk, on the edge of a bleak sea. Today World War One breaks out; all Europe is in tumult. And so are you, Rebecca; you are in labour, giving birth to a son, whom you have already, in successful anticipation of a male child, named Anthony. And since you are not married to the child's father, who is H. G. Wells, novelist, social philosopher, and someone else's husband; and since he is forty-seven, and you are twenty-one and in love with this older, married man, I suspect you need help. That is why I am writing to you. So much one novelist should do for another.

Your mother isn't here to look after you. She's a hundred miles away in London and, what's more, she isn't well. This may even be your fault. Mrs Fairfield is an intelligent and civilized woman and, though I don't suppose she'll be worrying about your sinfulness, she'll certainly be distressed by your folly in thus giving birth to an illegitimate child. No matter what you have to say about the absurdity of social censure, and the blow you are striking for women's personal, sexual and political liberty, she will not be convinced. Perhaps it's as well she's *not* here.

Your sister Letty would be with you but H.G. (who doesn't like her) said in his last letter she needn't be fetched: he himself could drive over from the marital home in Essex when the time came. And the time has come, and he hasn't driven over: he is in London delivering an article entitled (rashly, in retrospect) 'The War That Will End War'. And perhaps anyway his wife Amy/Jane wouldn't like it too much if he did drive over.

Your many friends and colleagues are too busy getting on with their London lives and careers and the general betterment of the world to pay much attention to you on this particular day of all days. And so you are left with a strange nurse, an unfamiliar midwife and a landlady you know all too well. (Does the latter guess who 'Mr West' really is? Probably. His face is everywhere these days, in magazines and newspapers. Mr Wells says this, Mr Wells says that . . .) These untrusted attendants no doubt seem to be running around talking about the war rather than concentrating properly on you. And you for the first time are frightened and in pain and feel yourself suddenly too young for your destiny. Your father died alone and in penury; perhaps you are to follow suit? Perhaps disgrace and loss are destined to press in and destroy you, as they destroyed him? In your head you hear the cat-calls of the crowd, as they mock and scorn a fallen woman. For that is what you are – a scarlet woman; an unmarried mother in an unforgiving decade. What have you done, albeit in the name of love, freedom, progress? What have you brought about? You will write about this guilt, this horror, this panic fear in *The Judge* and perhaps exorcize their demons a little. But just now, as pain follows helplessness, helplessness pain, they can only close in and torment you. This is the dark night of all your brilliant days.

Well, too late now. The baby which was all in the imagination is now all but here in the flesh. Only – how? How can something as large as a baby get through an opening as small as yours? You suffer the ordinary maternal conviction that you're going to be torn to bits. It's a puzzle, a perfectly horrible puzzle: obviously the baby has to get out, for if it stays inside you and grows, you will certainly burst – an even worse option. Yet, somehow, mothers live. Most of them. There is no way out for you, for the first time in your young life. The baby is barring the exits, as babies tend to do.

At this particular moment I suspect you need someone, anyone, to say, '*It is all going to be all right.*' I seem as well fitted as anyone to say it, being more than old enough in 1985 to be your 1914 mother; and your future and the world's to date lying mapped out before me, and my own early background and experience, though placed later in time, being not dissimilar to yours. I have the temerity to write to you – and temerity it is – only because you are so young. I would certainly not write to you in your later years about such subjects as love, life and married men. What could I know compared to you?

Let me say in my defence, in some small justification of this impertinence of mine, that I did grow up with you, in spite of the difference in generation. My grandmother, Susan Jepson, whose friend Violet Hunt was your friend, would speak of you often, with mingled awe and pity. She it was who said to me, unforgettably, 'Of course all us young women wanted to have babies by H.G. His brains and our beauty!' (I was young enough to be shocked, if only because I had believed her generation to be all impeccably respectable.) 'Mind you,' she added, 'it might have been his beauty and our brains. We never thought of that.' And then she said, 'Except of course for poor dear Rebecca, who just went ahead and did it.'

Poor dear Rebecca. Now look!

But *it's all going to be all right* – I promise. You did have a difficult early pregnancy, I know. But that was hardly the sign of a weak constitution: don't let it worry you. That was just the way you were running around the country conducting your affair, concealing your condition, hiding out here and there with H.G., snatching stolen nights, delicious afternoons, a week with complaisant friends here, a couple of days in lodgings there; lunching in smart restaurants with their very Edwardian, very discreet private rooms, where illicit literary afternoon love so often bloomed and flourished. Wonderful! – but not good for you. Wild sex and weak lungs – really! You did have tubercular trouble as a girl – you could hardly really be surprised, after all that carry-on, that you ended up ill and in a nursing home in the third month. But that weakness soon passed – well, it had to. Wells didn't like illness and you liked Wells – and the last months of the pregnancy, here in Hunstanton, have been peaceful enough, albeit boring. You are, I promise you, wonderfully fit and strong.

A pity you stopped work, though: stopped the articles and reviews for the *Clarion* and *Freewoman* – for which, although so young, you are already justifiably famous. You did keep the work going for a while, but then H.G. said (jokingly) that it was bad for the unborn baby, it would soften its bones. Rebecca, you shouldn't have listened. But don't bother about all that, nor its implications: I shouldn't have brought the matter up. Not now. Just breathe, breathe.

Relax, and the pain will be less. No one tells you that kind of thing in 1914. Women are supposed to bring forth in pain and anguish. No connection is made between mind and body. The word psychosomatic has not been coined. So I'm telling you now: can you hear me? Go with the pain, don't fight it. The maternal mortality rate is high, I know; the infant mortality rate appalling. But don't think of that either, it's not going to apply to you. And don't ask for chloroform until you really have to, Rebecca. This is the knowledgeable future talking. Anaesthetics hold things up. Labours are short, sharp, awful and over, or long, slow, awful and debilitating, then as now. And you'll need to mend quickly, after the birth. H.G. can't abide illness. It is a woman's chief duty, he remarks in his novel *Marriage*, to be *healthy*. 'Sick panthers,' he even wrote to you in your nursing home – he calls you Panther; you call him Jaguar – 'too easily become little Rebeccas.' And as a response to *that*, he fears, 'Jaguars have to become kind and attentive fathers, and then there can be no more love-making . . .' No, don't think of the implications of all *that*: he didn't quite mean it that way. Surely. Because if he did, this baby will not seal this love of yours, merely tear it apart –

Rebecca, there is life the other side of love. If only you could hear me. Perhaps you can? Perhaps through doubt, fear and pain comes a flickering sense of exultation, of future; the intimation that fate has you marked: that its plans are already made, unalterable. For this is the sense the future must have of the past, and it is this very awareness I am trying to broadcast back to you. *It is all going to be all right.* Your lungs will stand it, you won't tear apart, the pain will pass, and be forgotten. The shame will be faced and conquered. The baby is lovely, healthy, robust, will even grow up to be a writer. As is his father. As are you.

Breathe deeply. Compose yourself. You are not in as diffi-cult a position as many of your contemporaries. You are not helpless. You can (just) earn your own living, by writing. Your lover's wife, seen by a self-deluding posterity (and indeed by her husband, once she is dead) as a saint, for putting up with his infidelities and being so accommodating, even kind and chatty, to his lady friends, has no such option. She is complaisant because she has to be, she has no alternative: she does not *earn*. And so what if her husband wrongs her? Women in your day cannot divorce men for adultery: though men can divorce women for the offence. The double standard is enshrined in law. For your in-formation, the law is presently to change and wives will be permitted to take offence at infidelity, and start their own divorce proceedings. And then later changes will bring us up to our present, when human sexual behaviour is accepted with a shrug and a sigh; and matrimonial blame, for good or bad, no longer allocated by the courts. This one guilty – that one innocent. But the lot of the divorced and dependent wife is still not happy, in my day as in yours. Socially isolated, reduced in circumstances, relying for her comfort and security on the strength of a husband's guilt – except for the grudging assistance of an unwilling state. What has changed?

And back there at the beginning of the century, you, the mistress, unmarried and young, and she, the wife, married and in her middle years, both live in a milieu particularly distressing for women. You have no moral power. The trouble is that in the artistic, literary and intellectual circles in which you move, men have discovered Free Love, the Life Force, as the way forward to the future. Free Love for men, that is, just not for wives, daughters and sweethearts. Men look for, and claim, Life Mates, but marry pretty housewives, as usual. What's more, eugenics are all the rage – the my brains and your beauty syndrome – and beauty resides in the younger woman. So let's transmit the Life Force! It's our duty, not just our desire. Older women are having an even harder time of it than usual, as lofty statements all but drown the creaks and groans of riven homes.

Edith Nesbit, that enchanting writer of children's books and your contemporary, for many years housed and supported her husband's changing mistresses and occasional children at her Dymchurch home, by the sea. Visiting friends raised their eyebrows at an atmosphere described as 'sometimes strained', but it was the atmosphere, not the events, which seemed to upset the guests. Edith actually slammed doors and screamed behind them, inflamed no doubt by the fact that she was the one earning the money to keep the harem going. But it didn't help. Better to follow the example of Amy/Jane Wells. Edith learned in the end, and gave up, and smiled. Another complaisant wife. Poor dear Edith, my grandmother said, sighing.

And look what happened to Violet Hunt, your friend. She tried to claim her freedom, and ended up 'poor dear', as well. Violet used to move among artists, being the niece of Holman Hunt, and the model for the virgin in Burne-Jones's 'King Cophetua and the Beggar Maid', but then she took up with a literary man, Ford Madox Ford. He left his wife (more or less) and moved in with Violet, and she rashly allowed herself to be called Mrs Ford. (H.G. warned Violet against it: well, naturally. Supposing a trail of women started calling themselves Mrs Wells?) But Violet persisted in her folly and his wife, the legal Mrs Ford, sued. At the end of the lawsuit Violet had lost her reputation and her literary and artistic salon somehow evaporated. Poor dear Violet!

But a sense of injustice is no help at all in childbirth. I shouldn't be raising these matters either. Breathe, breathe, relax. You too are motivated by principle. You are very brave. You believe that to have a child by the man you love, married or not, is noble, right and glorious, and have acted on that belief. But it is not easy in this life to stand out for what is right, what is rational. Whatever made you think it would be? The good opinion of the world does matter. It is tangible in the same way the moon is tangible: it can't be touched but it's there, it shines: it lights the way on a dark night: without it you too easily stumble and fall. Courage is needed as you grope in the dark; hoping, against hope, for that very society which now derides and diminishes you, a better future, a freer, nobler existence. Conventional society sees only unhappy wives, bastard children: you in your way, Wells in his – for all that you, temporarily, are his victim – see a worthier, cleaner, finer (the adjectives of the time) shape of things to come, not just for you and your kind, but for everyone. And good for you! We owe our freedoms to your courage.

My grandfather, Edgar Jepson, mind you, thinks less well of you. You are too uppity, too bold, for his taste. You are a feminist and suffragist and therefore 'not impressed by what men think' – or so he complains in his *Autobiography of an Edwardian*. 'For the movement itself I have no sympathy,' he writes. 'Woman is the transmitter of the Life Force, man the instrument through which it attains its ends. It is not the business of women to govern countries.' You must not be surprised at the hostility you arouse in the bosoms of men writers, Rebecca. Not only because you are a suffragist and want to be allowed to vote, and govern countries, but because you are a critic, an essayist and a reviewer and are taking the bread out of their mouths, and, moreover, your fiction reviews are most upsettingly perspicacious. And my grandfather *is* a novelist, remember, and no doubt fears you. 'I do not think any female genius has eviscerated the unspeakable male so mercilessly,' protested a colleague, of your reviews. Unkind!

You were not only unkind, Rebecca, but rash in what, two years ago, in 1912, you had to say about Wells's new novel, *Marriage*. In this novel a young scientist marries an intelligent but idle young woman, who then proceeds to spend all his money, so that our hero has to abandon pure

33

research and work for a profit-making company – and only when she has abandoned home, furnishings, drapes and children at his behest, and gone off with our hero to the frozen wastes of Labrador to be purified of materialistic greed, home-making passion and maternalism, can they be truly lovers, truly soul-mates. (Oh, Rebecca, this does not augur well! What, no children, no curtains?) 'Of course,' you wrote in that all too trenchant, fatal review, 'Wells is the old maid amongst novelists: the sex obsession that lay clotted on *Ann Veronica* and *The New Machiavelli* like cold white sauce was merely old maid's mania: the reaction towards the flesh of a maid too long absorbed in airships and colloids.'

And there it was, for all the world to see. Wells, an old maid! Oh, thinking, feeling, ambitious, *young* Rebecca. You didn't, for one thing, in 1912, know what the flesh was, or how obsessive it could be (you know now); or how long it was since Mr Wells had in fact abandoned the celibate purity of *War of the Worlds* and *The Time Machine* and discovered 'sex obsession' in the person of Amber Reeve and others. And how, from then on, he was to be engaged in the process of justifying his own sexual behaviour, the random, fitful nature of his emotions, through his fiction – shrouding and muffling the sorry truth beneath a deceitful blanket of what passed for scientific thought, the progressive vision. And that he was going to carry on like this for the rest of his long, outspoken life. No. You just wrote the review and they published it, and here now, as a result, you lie in this white, high bed, transmitting the Life Force on Wells's behalf.

For Rebecca, if you, this swanning beauty, this rising intellectual star, say publicly of a notable man that he's an old maid, of course he'll have to prove to you and the world he's not. Of course. His richly sensuous nature will have to be made obvious to all around him. He'll disguise the fact to himself and you in any number of ways: he'll ask you round to meet him, define you as the New Woman, pay lip service to your fine independent spirit, then set you up to transmit the Life Force (which will also, he must hope, stop you writing) and then abandon you. Which your son Anthony is later to feel Wells was perfectly entitled to do. Hell hath no fury like a man pursued out of turn by a woman he no longer loves – and all men joining in their abhorrence of such an unnatural creature. And sons being men too.

Good radical separatist feminists of the eighties solve the problem of sons by simply not giving birth to them. They abort them. This is what Wells's fine, pure, clean, noble science has done for us all; but that's another story.

On the whole, Rebecca, the sad fact is, now as then, that men like women to appear and disappear, to exist and not exist, at their convenience, and are most put out when it doesn't happen. When former mistresses ring up in tears, when first wives insist on a roof over their heads, how great is male alarm and despondency, their sense of being hard-done-by! When men who have behaved badly are made to feel guilty the rafters echo with their rage. Hadn't you noticed? Not yet? You will, when arguments with H.G. about Anthony's school fees start. And if I generalize about men, tough titty! (Forgive me – I know it is an abominable phrase; and that this brave new world of ours is debased and degraded; but how well it fits the Kleinian view of things. Tough titty.)

Well, too late now. Having written such a review you should not have let Wells in the door. But you did. You should not have accepted the invitation to the rectory at Little Easton where Wells lived with his wife Amy/Jane. You should not have accepted her hospitality and generosity and then betrayed them. You should have known better. But you didn't. You should not have had an affair with another woman's husband. But you did. You should have taken with many pinches of salt H.G.'s claim that he and she were no longer lovers. (Amazing how naïvely posterity as well accepts this claim. It is normal for married men to say this to their mistresses and just occasionally no doubt it is true. But only occasionally.) But how are you to know things like this? We in our day have *Cosmopolitan* and *Woman's Own* to tell us: a hundred quizzes on the human psyche, innumerable investigations into the hearts and psycho-sexual pathology of man at our fingertips; we know, or think we know, what to expect of the world of suitors, lovers, husbands – you have none of this information. You live in a world of dignity and innocence, with only a serious novel or two to help you know what's what, and the whispered conversations of friends to enlighten you.

Listen to me, Rebecca, back in 1912, when you are still your own woman. I'm trying to tell you something. You have so much to lose. Don't let him in the door. Don't! H. G. Wells may know the world, may see the coming inevitability of the World State and so forth, may overwhelm you with the sweep and breadth of his mind – but he doesn't know himself. Are you deaf? Can you hear nothing but the singing in your ears, the music of celestial choirs? Can you feel nothing? No prudence, no remorse? As those strong fingers, potent with so much written eloquence, turn your soft face up to meet his – no, wait, wait: he's very short; you're a fine, robust young woman: omit 'up' – the bristly moustache (oh, unkind to think of it!) brushes your skin, the full sensuous lips meet yours . . . and then, and then . . . Oh, really, Rebecca! Was it for this your mother reared you, ending in this leaping of a forbidden baby in the all-too-ready womb, the childbirth in Hunstanton, as the Life Force sweeps you off your feet?

Cold White Sauce. Unforgivable! Love her and leave her. That'll teach her.

Too late!

> I like the feel of you
> I like the noises you make
> I love your faults
> I love your voice
> I love your truth
> I love your affections
> I love you . . .

Wells wrote that to you in a letter in early 1914. He loves you! But careful, careful! He wrote so many letters to so many people, not just to you. One or the other to someone or other was bound to turn out like that. Was it you he *meant*? Rebecca, before it's too late! This man is forty-seven: he has discovered he's mortal and is desperate; his pen outruns his brain, his common sense his feelings. Part of you must know all this: can't afford not to know it. But too late now. It's 5 August 1914. You can't afford to know it, just at the moment. Very well. Put it from your mind. Lie back on your feather pillows, in their stiff white cotton slips, the draw-sheet ready, the midwife back from the kitchen; lie back, and think, if you can, of love.

But how can you, for more than a minute or two? I know, I know. Here you must lie in dreary Hunstanton – you, accustomed to cities: to Edinburgh, where you were reared; to London, where you had such early, instant success – because this is where your lover has decided you will live! And he is supposed to be here, and he isn't.

The rhythm of the pains gets more insistent, your body convulses – what is this; is this the Life Force? The light of the sun spreading a monstrous flower of pain against burning, closed eyelids: is this your destiny? Oh yes indeed, what else, indeed it is; your body is not yours: they are right in what they say: this is indeed the Life Force, and it's killing you. (It's not, you know. Merely the transition from First to Second Stage. You know so little, so very little: terms such as First Stage, Second Stage, Three Fingers Dilated, are not in common currency, not even in the midwife's handbook: not fit knowledge for a woman, on 5 August 1914 – midnight has come and gone – for how can the soul, the spirit, triumph if the body is too well understood?) All is ignorance, all is faith: all is terror: and you are mystified, and you are hurting, and all you understand is pain, anguish, punishment, and the war is breaking out and your lover is not even here, and it's Too Late!

Push, Rebecca, push, and good for you! Of course you did all these things. Lied, deceived, loved and lost. I'm glad you were deaf to common sense, conventional morality, and

indifferent to – though always conscious of – social disgrace. The Life Force was with you and the baby was – is,
for here he is: pain stops: reason asserts itself – worth it all!
New life, new energy. Perfect, and perfectly helpless. There
is something here that will love and not argue – at least not
for a time. Something which can be the flawless recipient of
love, as no grown man can ever be.

There now, it's over. Lie back, be well, and now you can
indeed think of love. The church bells are ringing; and if not
because Anthony is born but because war has broken out
and the whole nation must be roused to hate, never mind.

How is it possible for people to live and love and be happy
in such a wicked world? Or, conversely, how can the world
be peaceful and happy, when it has such wicked people in
it? Forget it. Go to sleep.

Dear Rebecca,

Well, this is better. The baby is two days old and thriving, and your sister Letty has turned up to keep you company. Letty is seven years your senior. She has already qualified as a doctor and is now studying law; she cannot bear mess and muddle. She will end up as a senior civil servant, as renowned in her field as you in yours. You describe her in *The Fountain Overflows* with mixed compassion and acerbity. Letty (or so they said at school) has a mind like a razor – yours being rather more like a high-powered circular saw, which at the moment is sending out (according to Letty) even more muddling and messy flurries of sawdust than usual. Letty looks with mingled distaste and admiration at the bundle which is the fruit of your and H.G.'s sexual mess and muddle and hands it back to Nurse, who takes it away. And thus, I imagine, the conversation goes:

LETTY: Is that all?
YOU: What do you mean, 'all'?

LETTY: I thought it was meant to be a special baby. It looks like any other to me.

YOU: Well it's not. You know nothing about babies, Letty.

LETTY: Neither do you. Well, he will just have to grow up to be Prime Minister if he is to justify all this disgrace and inconvenience. I suppose H.G. hasn't been near you?

YOU: He will come as soon as he can.

LETTY: So you say. Well, we won't go into all that now. You are on your sick bed. Mother says she'll come when she's feeling a little stronger. She hasn't been well.

YOU: I suppose she's in a terrible wax.

LETTY: Of course.

YOU: I love him, Letty.

LETTY: And mother loved father, and where did that get her?

YOU: This is entirely different.

LETTY: So you say. Is that the baby crying?

YOU: Yes. It's natural for babies to cry.

LETTY: Only if they're neglected, surely. Are you sure the nurse is a good type? She has a coarse face.

YOU: She was well recommended.

LETTY: Ah, but by whom? And did she know your situation? You will be very easily taken advantage of, Cicily. I hope you didn't accept a written reference.

YOU: Yes, I did.

LETTY: But they are usually forged. Don't you know that?

YOU [*weakly*]: She seems perfectly pleasant.

LETTY: I would have thought efficiency a better recommendation than amiability, Cicily.

YOU: Please don't call me Cicily, call me Rebecca.

LETTY: You were born Cicily, and that's what you'll always be to me. And to mother. I think she was very hurt when you changed your name. In fact I think it contributed greatly to her illness. But that's you, isn't it! Going your own way. Of course, you'll have to tell the servants you're the baby's aunt.

YOU: I don't think the nurse, for one, will believe that, Letty.

LETTY: Women of that class, of low intelligence and no breeding, have short memories. That's why they're so hard to train. For once the moral and mental deficiency of the lower classes works in our favour. We can't have a baby in our family described as a bastard.

YOU: Please don't even say that word. Use 'love child' instead. Because that's what he is. That's why he's so beautiful.

LETTY: Facts are facts. In law he's a bastard, and both of you will be unacceptable in decent society unless you pretend otherwise. It's the pretence that's important. Everyone will *know*, but as long as you pay-lipservice to ordinary standards, all will be well.

YOU: But that's hypocrisy!

LETTY: Never mind. You must think of your baby. You don't want him mocked and jeered at, despised and derided, by every guttersnipe that passes by.

YOU: That's hardly going to happen to H. G. Wells's baby!

LETTY: H. G. Wells may make quite a stir in some circles, but he cuts very little ice outside London, I can tell you. Has the baby stopped crying?

YOU: Yes.

LETTY: I wonder why. Perhaps the nurse is feeding him

opium? They do, you know. The poor little creature. You should never have taken a written testimonial!

But at least the tensions Letty brings into Brig-y-don are familiar and make everything seem more like home. All the same, the fact that the baby is not going to stay a babe-in-arms for ever, will not just exist as the living symbol of a great love, but will grow up to be a thinking, feeling person, and will have to bear, along with you, the disgrace of his illegitimacy, begins to dawn on you. What have you done? Fortunately, Mrs Townshend is also on hand to comfort and console you. She has come at Wells's bidding and for this you are more than grateful. Mrs Townshend is wise, witty, in her forties and a friend of the Wellses, man and wife. It was in her home in Earls Court that on many occasions you met and embraced the baby's father, and Mrs Townshend feels, and rightly, rather responsible for what has happened now. (I hope she feels a little bad about Mrs Wells, but I'm not sure that she does. Wells's convenience somehow so much out-weighs Mrs Wells's discomfiture.) Thus the conversation goes:

MRS T: What a beautiful, beautiful baby. So like his father, but yet not too like!

YOU: I hope he grows up to be tall.

MRS T: I'm sure he will. And I know H.G. will be here to see you as soon as he possibly can. I saw him in London and he said just that, and asked me to come down and make sure all was well. He's so pleased and happy and proud: he's overtipping everyone as if he'd come into a fortune.

You should have seen the expression on the cabbie's face as he drove away!

YOU: I do understand he's very busy. Even more so than usual. He has the birth-pangs of the World State to midwife, after all. How strange, but very apt, that both should be born on the same day, his child and his prophetic child, both conceived in the tumult of passion – love is like war, don't you think?

MRS T [*cautiously*]: For some!

And if Mrs Townshend looks around the bleak furnished rooms of Brig-y-don and is appalled at what Wells has brought you to, she tries not to let her feelings show. This is scarcely the time. But Brig-y-don! Hunstanton! A hundred miles from London, family, friends: another hundred miles from Wells himself. A place picked, apparently, with a pin! Picked certainly in the interests of discretion; but picked also, she must be tempted to think, for the greater discomfiture of poor you. For who can you possibly talk to here? You, who are used to literary conversation, wit, good times, general admiration and intellectual endeavour, now must look out over a dull suburban street in one of the dullest towns in the country, and nurse your baby and hold your tongue, until such times as your lover turns up, with news and views of the outside world. You must now depend upon him not just for things emotional and practical, but intellectual as well. You know well enough what she is thinking. Your heart flutters helplessly. You wave your pretty hands and begin to weep a little.

MRS T [*half joking, half not*]: Rebecca, I have found you out!

You are not a bachelor-woman at all. You are a slave to love, like the rest of us. Whatever will Wells say! He would like you to be polygamous, I know: he will be disappointed to discover you are not; we will have to break it to him tactfully.

YOU [*impassioned*]: Break away! I hardly care. H.G. is like any other man ever born. He reserves the right to infidelity for himself and then, being truly modern – in other words, hypocritical – offers that right in theory to all the women he knows, but only in theory. Being himself such a monster of jealousy and possessiveness, he is furiously angry if any woman dares reveal the same qualities in herself. I see through him, don't think I don't!

MRS T: I am sorry you have had to discover all this so young.

YOU [*collapsing, weeping*]: What have I done, Mrs Townshend? What am I to do now? I know these things about H.G. but it doesn't stop me loving him, and needing him, and waiting for him. Waiting, all the time. I mark his visits in my diary with a cross. Well, at least now I have something more of his than just a few ink marks on paper: I have a baby, Wells's baby, and when I am not utterly miserable I am so very happy!

> [*You weep: you are very agitated. Mrs Townshend calls the nurse to bring the baby; together they put the baby to your full white breast.*]

MRS T: There now, that is a delightful sight!

YOU: But Nurse was going to hand-rear the baby. I can't possibly suckle him myself. I have to work, to earn; I have my career. I have to get out of this dreadful, dreadful place – how can I if I don't earn? Please take the baby away: the milk hasn't come in yet. Better it doesn't. Because if it does, and then I have to stop, I'll get an ulcer, Letty says so: it will become infected and I'll die and what will happen to the baby? I will not have it looked after by Mrs Wells. She'll smother it. And my mother isn't well enough and Letty will just put it in a home for unfortunates!

MRS T: Please calm down, Rebecca. You *will* suckle the baby: suckling is a great calmant. H.G. doesn't like it when you are excited and tearful and reproachful. Think of that!

YOU [*when you have calmed down*]: I do try. It is so difficult. H.G. is so good a talker he makes black seem white and then what can one do but scream? And then one gets into the habit –

MRS T: Quite so. Now hold the baby like this: its head like this, the nipple like that. There!

[*The baby succeeds, sucks, is properly gratified.*]

YOU: The little angel! But what a funny feeling it is for me, like being an animal! But I suppose I will get used to it.

[*When the baby is suckling happily and you are feeling calmer, Mrs Townshend continues.*]

MRS T: He admires you very much, Rebecca. He won't abandon you; he won't leave you here. I'll see that he doesn't. You and the baby must live somewhere more sensible, I do agree.

YOU: But how does he admire me?

MRS T: He thinks you're very clever. He even liked your book on Henry James. You would have to be very special to him to write a book on Henry James and have it liked!

YOU: 'Liked' is too strong a word. For one so young and wrong-headed, is what he said to me, for someone who so foolishly believes in Art, Truth, Beauty, Literature and so forth, it was 'not too bad'. He could scarcely say otherwise, but he did his best. He hates my writing. He thinks I am so rich as to be indigestible; that I am over-emotional, that I shape nothing but amble on. I don't amble on as much as he does, that's for sure. Well, he shan't have it all his own way. I think his writing is so dry as to be inedible! But I wish he was here. He must come soon –the longer he stays away the more justified Letty will be in suspecting his motives, and the more unforgiving Mother will be. Mrs Townshend, now had you thought of this: he doesn't like Letty, and he doesn't like my mother –

MRS T: Naturally. Men don't 'like' where they're not approved of.

YOU: But men make such laws of their whims! He should keep his dislike to himself, don't you think? I would never say to him, 'I don't like your mother, H.G. She has this quality or the other which makes her unlikeable, unacceptable to me! Keep her away from me!' Would I? Would any woman?

MRS T: No.

YOU: Then why do men? Why do men place their likes and dislikes above women's actual needs and requirements?

MRS T: Rebecca, the baby has lost hold!

YOU: Oh, so he has!

MRS T: Try and talk a little less: just *be* a little more.

YOU: Now you sound like H.G.

Presently you sleep. At least you *can* rest, and are encouraged to do so. You will not be expected to put a foot to
the floor for at least three weeks after the birth. Mothers in
your day are not. (Those at any rate who can afford to rest:
washer-women and such like must no doubt be up and
back at the tub, or whatever, to feed the extra mouth, pretty
smartish.)

Letty and Mrs Townshend take tea together, and get on
as well as can be expected of two women who are both
very fond of you indeed, but have nothing else in
common. Letty thinks Mrs Townshend has helped land
you in your present predicament by encouraging your
unfortunate liaison with Wells, and Mrs Townshend,
who has spent a lot of time listening to Wells abusing
your family, sees Letty as being on that stuffy, morbid,
life-and-love-negating side of things so disliked by Wells and
all forward-thinking people.

Tip-tap on the front door! Who can it be, come to Brig-y-
don, Victoria Avenue, on 8 August 1914? Mrs Crown, the
landlady, goes to see. In your bedroom on the first floor you
wait, expectant. Can it be, surely it is, the baby's father?
Here at last? Quick, the comb! A dab of rouge; forbidden,
secret. How do you look now? Your dark soft hair flowing
over white pillows, your strong face grave and pale – not
wronged, Rebecca, the expression should not be wronged,
that's not going to help anyone: just *serious* – your intelligent
eyes large and glowing with – what, erotic love, maternity
fulfilled? . . . well, never mind: he'll read into them what he
wants, not what's there – let's just say expectancy. In other
words you look wonderful and you know it, and the sun

pours in, and Mrs Townshend has put flowers in a vase –
Letty said flowers were a waste of money; she would! –
and surely now this must, this must be H.G.! He will stand
there in the door and laugh, and it will be as if a strong
wind blows in with him; the wind of the future, whistling
through the bead curtains, bending Mrs Crown's aspi-
distras in all directions, all but whisking her antimacassars
right away. Standing here in the flesh will be the spirit of
things to come, for all he is the housekeeper's son, his
physical existence so mundane, the body short and
rotund, the moustache greying, the voice squeaky – but
the eyes so bright, the vitality so abundant, who cares!
And the mind, you always think, the extraordinary mind
– which fears nothing, faces everything; there is such
exhilaration here in the adventure of thought, such a
surplus of animation and generosity! Of course it seeps
through to the body; makes it what it is, seductive, ener-
getic, unstoppable. If young women lie down in the path
of this energy, what do they expect? They will be steam-
rollered! All this energy of mind must take some kind of
physical form: overflowing as pot plants overwatered
overflow on to polished surfaces – the phallus stirs, leaps,
hardens, procreates – this is Wells!

Of course, Rebecca, in spite of all advice to the contrary,
from present, past and future, you will open the door to
him, whenever and if he be so inclined to knock upon it.
The fact is that you are amazingly, wonderfully privileged.
(Yes, yes, I know he is too, with you: but it's different. The
mantle of the Muse falls on you; the mantle of the Future
upon him. There are more like you: almost no one like him.

He is rarer stuff.) To give pleasure to a god is no small thing, no matter how clay-like his feet.

Wells wrote to you, Rebecca, of your delicious bed, and of his longing to be in it, and there's a whole lifetime's worth of gratification for any ordinary person. *Your delicious bed.* A letter to fold and open and fold again and place beneath a pillow and sleep upon and dream upon, and live the life of a recluse thereafter, if that is what fate (or Wells) requires of you.

But then, of course, you're no ordinary person. Such weighty matters, such impressive events, you feel to be no more than your due. (This much youth and beauty will do for a girl – make her uppity enough, even leaving out talent, ability, intellect, those other purely asexual qualities which in fact do make it no more than you deserve.) Your delicious bed! What pleasure! What greater pleasure can any of us have, than to love and be loved in return? If only temporarily.

Your bedroom door finally opens. And no, after all that, it isn't Wells. It is only Mrs Crown, having taken a letter from the milkman. And yes, it is from your own true love. You open the letter. You keep your face calm. (You are good at dissembling. You had an excellent training in it as a child.)

'Oh, from Mr West,' you say. 'He is to be a war correspondent, Mrs Crown, and go to the Front. What a terrible thing war is. How it tears families apart!'

Does Mrs Crown raise her eyebrows? Probably! The working classes are not so deficient in intellect as you and your sister have been brought up to believe.

[*Mrs Crown finally goes. You call for Mrs Townshend.*]

YOU: A letter from H.G.! A lovely letter. He says he is radiant. He says he is overtipping everyone. (You were right about the cabbie!) He says he is delighted to have a man-child, and if he is busy it is only because he is making a better world for the baby. And he most tremendous loves me.

MRS T: Of course he does.

YOU: Mrs Townshend, he has loved other women most tremendous and now no longer does.

MRS T: He is older and more serious now, Rebecca.

But Mrs Townshend can hardly quite believe what she says. What a mess, she thinks. What a mess! And is quite cross with Wells for a moment, but on the other hand he is a Great Man, and a lot must be excused a Great Man – and perhaps it is better to be half loved by Wells than properly and fully loved by anyone else in the world. Oh, envied Rebecca!

For Wells, everyone who's anyone agrees, is a most remarkable man, a latter-day prophet. And he is so hopeful, so somehow nice. The pair of you are. You envisage a future which goes on forever, which little by little must bring itself to Utopia: you see stupidity and ignorance as responsible for most human ills and look forward to a time when knowledge and science will illuminate all the dark corners of the human heart, and abolish them: you live, in other words, in pre-Belsen, pre-Hiroshima days, and can afford hope. You, Rebecca, in fact are more at home in the dark corners than Wells. You have a richer, almost satanic imagination, a nightmarish knowledge, gained as a child.

A child who has eaten too many cream éclairs for nursery tea, and then alone in the black and lonely night, is flung into the mire of her own terror, her own outrageous passions. The hint of nightmare will be there in all your writings: in Wells there is a benignity, a thorough-going realism, practical, useful. You could burn a volume of yours to raise the Devil; burn a Wells novel and all you could do with the flames would be to keep the cold away. But that's something.

[*The baby's crying. Letty brings it in.*]

LETTY: Nurse had her finger in the baby's mouth. I'm sure she hasn't washed it! You will have to get rid of her, Cicily. I don't like the way she looks at me. Perhaps she's recognized your paramour as Mr Wells?

YOU: Don't say paramour. Say lover, say 'passionate friend'. You are sometimes so Scottish, Letty.

LETTY: I am not in the least ashamed of it. If you hadn't got yourself into this mess you would be at the Front, the first woman war correspondent. How proud Mother would be of you then.

YOU: Don't think I haven't thought of that. I know what I've given up. But this feeling is so rich and deadly, Letty, you have no idea. Love and motherhood and babies! It's all rushed in on me so suddenly!

LETTY: Good heavens, listen to you! Perhaps you should have persisted and been an actress after all, and disgraced us that way, instead of this.

YOU [*weeping again*]: What about my career? What's to become of me? What have I done?

LETTY: Those are Mother's lines, Cicily –

YOU: Rebecca –

LETTY: Cicily. Of course you have given up any hope you ever had of making a proper marriage. You will never be able to entertain as other people do. Look what happened to Violet Hunt. What an irresponsible woman!

Poor dear Violet. You contemplate her fate. Lost her reputation!

YOU [*pulling yourself together*]: But this is absurd, Letty! Insanity! A million young men are already marching off to war. The mad old generals can't wait to get them to the Front. Who cares a fig in 1914 about reputation?

LETTY: Everyone.

She's right. Not everyone who's anyone, of course: but everyone who isn't anyone. Nurses, cooks, landladies, teachers. Rebecca, what have you done!

YOU: Letty, you really think Wells is just another husband, don't you, off on yet another affair with a girl young enough to be his daughter.

LETTY: Yes.

YOU: It isn't like that.

LETTY: So you say.

YOU: There is something special about me.

LETTY: And the lunatic asylums are full of Napoleon Bonapartes and Marie Antoinettes. I know.

YOU: It's just I have to learn to take love lightly. It's so difficult.

LETTY [*incensed*]: Oh, the beast! The vile seducer! Why

should you take love lightly! How can you have a man's baby and not be serious about it?

She's right of course. Rebecca, you do take Wells seriously, and must not. Not only does he take love lightly, but he is proud of doing so. Writing about the difference between his own attitude to extra-marital affairs and that of his colleague Hubert Bland (E. Nesbit's husband), your lover observes, 'We were in diametrically antagonistic schools. He thought it made a love affair more exciting and important if one might be damned for it, and I could not believe these pleasant intimacies could ever bring real damnation to anyone . . .'

'Pleasant intimacies', Rebecca. That's all.

'. . . Bland was sincerely disgusted at my disposition to take the moral fuss out of his darling sins. My impulses were all to get rid of the repressions of sexual love, minimize its importance and subordinate this stress between men and women as agreeably as possible to the business of mankind.'

Well, my dear, no doubt he warned you, as many a husband or live-in lover warns his wife (or whatever) today. 'We will have an open relationship. We won't be hypocritical. We will each go our own ways, if occasion arises; returning refreshed to the marriage (or whatever) bed.' Oh yes, she cries, why yes, my darling, hardly hearing, so deep in love is she. And what happens? He returns refreshed: she returns weeping. I know, I know: everything is so different now: it is the woman who chooses and disposes, not the man – she has the upper hand sexually: in theory, I daresay, but it's not the tale I hear at the hairdressers. Now as then.

Rebecca, in your review of *Marriage* – I am sorry to go

back to it, but I am afraid we have to – you mocked H.G.'s love scenes most acutely, most correctly:

Mr Wells's mannerisms are more infuriating than ever in *Marriage*. One knows at once that Marjorie is speaking in a crisis of chastity when she says at regular intervals, 'Oh, my dear! Oh my dear!' or at moments of ecstasy, 'Oh my *dear*! My *dear*!'

Truth makes bad art. I have no doubt Amber Reeve (your predecessor-but-one in Wells's affections) said 'my *dear*' quite often. And so no doubt did Elizabeth, writer of *Elizabeth and Her German Garden* – my grandmother's friend, your predecessor. You shouldn't have mocked. He has had his revenge now. You want him more than he wants you. Oh, my dear, you say weeping. My *dear*.

If only he were here at this moment so you could say it! But he will be soon. Yes he will. Mrs Townshend says so. Take no notice of Letty.

Sleep now. I will write to you again tomorrow.

Rebecca West *c*. 1914

H. G. Wells *c*.1920

Left: Brig-y-don, Victoria Avenue, Hunstanton, Norfolk
Middle: Easton Glebe, near Dunmow, Essex
Bottom: Rebecca with Ford Madox Ford *c.*1914

Opposite, top: President Truman presenting Rebecca with the Achievement Award Certificate in Washington in the late 1940s
Opposite, bottom: Rebecca after her investiture as Dame Commander, Order of the British Empire, on 10 February 1959. On her left is her husband, Henry Andrews; on her right, the economist Roy Harrod

Dame Rebecca West on her way to the Old Bailey to give evidence at the *Lady Chatterley's Lover* trial in October 1960

Dear Rebecca,

Better still! Anthony is five days old; your mother has wired to say she'll be at Hunstanton station at 2.30, and Letty has agreed to meet the train. You will feel much easier in your mind once your mother has seen and held the baby: he will seem more real and less a figment of your over-heated imagination, your dream of Wells. 'Seeing the baby' is an important ceremony for relatives and friends, as if only thus can the newly arrived spirit be anchored in flesh and blood. A second's glimpse will do: the brief pulling away of the shawl to reveal the tiny face is all that's needed. The baby is 'seen'. What your mother will *say* is, of course, a different matter; but I promise you will end up on good terms, and not succumb to Wells's view of her as a 'man-hater', although it will always distress you.

You are not alone. The male habit of accusing women of hating them has not diminished over the decades: on the contrary. As a female sin it looms large in the minds of those men who can most justly be accused of mistreating women. It is a symptom of male guilt, Rebecca, and when Wells abuses your mother like that, you should remember it. Freud's notions of the phenomenon of projection, although formulated, are not yet ordinary received wisdom, so let me pass them on to you. Loosely, that whatever sin, fault, or shortcoming another accuses you of, is what that other is most nervous of finding in himself. When he cries 'man-hater' he says of himself 'woman-hater'. When he cries 'infidelity!' – my dear, ask where he was last night.

Of course Wells wants to discredit your mother. They're the same age. She knows too much. Take no notice!

But what is this? Here comes Mrs Townshend in hat and coat, saying she must be off. It won't do for her to meet your mother.

YOU: Please don't go! You keep us all cheerful. I know mother will love you. How could she not!

MRS T: Very easily, my dear. Your mother can hardly be expected to think kindly of me, since I think so kindly of Wells. She will believe I should have saved you from all this. I did, after all, receive the pair of you in my house, and in her view, naturally, I shouldn't have given you this encouragement. I see you as a woman sees another woman; she sees you as a mother sees a daughter, as is only right and proper. I see that you and Wells are right together; that you make a very proper pair, in spite of the difference in your ages. I see not his brains and your beauty, as your mother will assume I do – his age and your youth – but his charm and your brain, and she won't see this latter as anything remarkable, being used to it. But we all marvel at it. You are very young and very pretty, but so are a thousand other girls to whom Mr Wells is not in the least attracted.

YOU: I hope to heaven he sees more in me than my brain. He will have to, because it is so remarkably sluggish at the moment. I feel somewhere between a cow and a cabbage. Is this what childbearing does to women? Do you think I will ever recover?

My own view, Rebecca, is that it takes all of two years.

MRS T: It will take a month or so, I daresay, and then you will be back to normal.

YOU: Mrs Townshend, it is such a frightening thought. I will never be free again! Wherever I go I will have to have servants and nurses and chaperones: I will somehow have to have the money to provide for them.

MRS T: That is the least of your worries. I am sure Wells will not let you starve.

YOU: His wife will wish me to. She is such an expense to him, forever buying houses and altering them. He is a free spirit and she tries to tie him down with bricks and mortar and domesticity.

MRS T: That is as much his doing as hers, Rebecca, and you know it. He likes to be comfortable, and he is a married man.

[*She is warning you. She is right to. You don't like it. She prepares to go.*]

YOU: He is married in name only.

Oh heavens, thinks Mrs Townshend, what is to become of

you! Presently you will want Wells to forsake Amy/Jane and marry you, and that will never happen. She is right, Rebecca. Writers have talismans, by the grace of which they believe they work: some have desks they must sit at, others views they must look at; Wells has his wife. The writer, perceiving that his gift is the product of some rare and chancy combination of circumstances, fears any radical change in those circumstances, lest the gift desert him. Try and understand this, and not be too hurt by it.

Wells laughs and bounces and talks and argues and no one would insult him by suggesting he was just simply unhappily married. The conventional wisdom, among his friends, is that it is impossible for a man of such talent and vitality to confine himself sexually to one woman and that if his genius requires the sacrifice of a virgin or two then that is a small matter. They just wish he'd try and be more tactful about it. Wells's enemies maintain he is a philandering rogue who writes indecent novels; the upstart son of a housekeeper who by his conduct is bringing socialism in general, and Fabianism in particular, into disrepute. You, Rebecca, being his lover, are alone in understanding that he is unhappily married to a woman who does not properly appreciate him either sexually or mentally. No doubt, in conversation with you, he exaggerates her failings and his own wretchedness, as erring husbands will, but it is true enough in essence. It is an ambition properly felt by all young female creatures, this desire to make the unhappy male happy, to somehow make up by sheer force of love, by proximity of youth and generosity of spirit and flesh, for all the unhappiness, humiliation and misfortune the object of their love has ever endured.

But you see, Rebecca, it can't be done. The young female gets chewed up and mangled in the teeth of male habit and sheer practicability. Love can't make an unhappy man happy (or not for long) any more than it can stop an alcoholic drinking. Good intentions and resolution fade and the bad habit reasserts itself. Wells is not unhappy *because* he is married to Amy/Jane. He could cure the symptom – his wife – but not the cause – no doubt his mother, she being too deeply entwined in his being for eradication. And somewhere in his heart he knows it.

Your mother knows this too. She has had experience of unhappy men. Her lover and husband, your father – rake, gambler, profligate, all charm and socialist principle – who once held George Bernard Shaw in argument till midnight and won – kept her forever tossed on seas of passion and despair. His moods alternated, seesaw-like, out of spurts of exuberant, exhilarating energy into silent, staring sullenness, until he finally crawled up out of one of the fits of depression and went for ever, leaving her with three young children and no money. Of course she doesn't want the same for you. He was, you once said, 'a glorious father and no father at all'. And here you are, repeating patterns, giving the same kind of father to your own baby, clinging to the same hope, that one day it will be all right. It won't be, but, do believe me, it will be the making of you. You will succeed where your mother failed. Love killed her in the end: she died ill and defeated in her fifties. But you are stronger; your mother gave you a better inheritance; you will live, undefeated, gaining strength where hers was sapped, into vigorous old age, and the respect of an entire nation.

In the meantime, you're hardly twenty, Mother's coming, Mrs Townshend's going and you're frightened.

YOU: Mother's bound to be in a mood. Do stay.
   [*But Mrs Townshend won't be moved.*]
YOU: Please, at least do speak to Nurse before you go. Letty thinks she's feeding the baby syrup from her thumb to make him sleep, and of course she mustn't.
MRS T: Syrup's not such a bad thing, Rebecca.
YOU: Oh, but it is!
MRS T: The philosopher Herbert Spencer says it's good for children to eat sweet things. It sweetens their nature.
YOU: But that isn't why she does it. She does it so she can have an easy life. She does it from base motives.
MRS T: And the baby will respond to the motive, not the syrup?
YOU: Of course.

The cabbie knocks at the door. It's time for Mrs Townshend to go for her train. Of course, she can afford to take a hansom cab. Your mother will walk from the station, though Letty will long for a cab and try to persuade her to take one. But Mrs Fairfield doesn't like to waste money. She is accustomed to frugality; she enjoys it. She, a woman of good family, and of intelligence, sensitivity and talent, chose to marry the wrong man, and ended, if not in the gutter – it being too well swept, fastidious, intelligent and cultured a place to be called that – at any rate in threadbare clothes and well-polished shoes worn so thin they let in water. Perhaps it suited her? Perhaps thus she could concentrate on the pleasures of the mind rather than those of the flesh? And if the children went to school looking extremely odd, because there wasn't the money to make them look ordinary, at least they concentrated on their lessons. They knew they would have to save themselves since there was no one else to save them. And what control does a woman have over her own destiny, was Mother's argument, if she can't support herself, if she isn't educated? None!

On the other hand, Mother understands love. 'You meet,' says Mother, asked why she married her husband, why she stayed with him, 'and there's an end to it.' Why can't she understand that now you and Wells have met, there's the end to that, likewise? And to all possible comment from her? But that's not how mothers see it; nor, when Anthony has grown, how you'll see his life either. Nor how my mother sees my life; nor how I see my children's lives. Nothing changes, however hard we all try, in this particular respect. Mothers cannot refrain from comment, even when it is most uncalled for, most distressing.

So Mrs Townshend goes, and hastens home, composing a letter to Wells in her mind, which she is to post soon. She will have to be tactful – and is. Wells, as a novelist, is supposed to understand the human heart, but clearly understands not a beat of yours, or he would not assume you will make do for ever with rented rooms and a lover who appears at discreet intervals. Wells cannot, simply, do nothing: but if nobody prods him, that is exactly what he will do. Your good friend Mrs Townshend, as the LNER train rumbles London-wards, no doubt wonders why it is always left to her to clear up other people's messes.

Mrs Crown opens the front door to your mother. You hear the familiar footsteps coming lightly up the stairs, as you so often heard them through your childhood; coming with whatever it was going to be: whether reassurance or admonition, glasses of water, cough syrup, or unexpected scoldings, or the sudden blaze of healthy light into an unhealthy nightmare. Or sometimes, as mothers will, bringing nightmare into serenity, traumatizing the child with the sudden shock of the mother's grief, or anxiety, or rage, standing there weeping at the end of the bed as if she were the child, and you the mother. Mothers are all mixed: a paper bag of liquorice sweets. Put your child's hand in, and heaven knows what you'll bring out!

You have arranged your hair to good effect – but have left off the rouge: good. Mrs Fairfield is not one to approve of female vanity and affectation: a woman, she thinks in her good Scottish way, is what she is, and should hope to be appreciated for her mind and her character and not her looks. (Ha bleeding ha, then as now.) Nurse has handed you the baby and withdrawn. (Please do smile at Nurse whenever you can, Rebecca. It is no use looking sulkily and suspiciously at her. It won't make her behave better: merely dislike you more.) Anthony is sleeping soundly and peacefully, with that rapt returned-to-the-womb look that well-fed babies have whenever and if ever their digestions leave them in peace. Lift the shawl. See! The red pressure marks on the back of his neck which worried you yesterday are fading fast; the spotty rash which affected his cheeks and chin have altogether subsided. There is, true, a slight stickiness around his mouth. Syrup! Now don't get agitated. Just wipe it away with your lace hankie. (Your baby pre-dates tissues by some fifty years.) Lie back against your pillow. Breathe deeply. Your heart, I'm afraid, is beating almost as fast as if it were Wells you were expecting. And in walks Mama.

Mama is a 'little brown bird of a woman' – according to Wells, who also accuses her of intensely and generically hating men. But since Wells also claims your mother comes from the West Indies and the only possible evidence I can see for this is your own strong, dark face, which I suppose he might wish to see as romantically un-British, I take him as a dubious witness who only ever sees what he wants to see, in which of course he is much like anyone else. Myself, being no doubt equally given to wishful thinking, I prefer to see her as the mother in *The Fountain Overflows*, your obliquely autobiographical novel – the brave, witty and sensitive woman with the beautiful voice, always more beautiful when she is distressed, 'rising to a thin silver thread, rather high, spinning from behind her high forehead: but who also [seems] to grow thinner at such times, and ugly, her eyes protruding'. A woman 'who could not dress herself to go out of her house tidily enough to avoid attracting hostile stares; who could not speak to strangers except with such naivety that they thought her a simpleton, or with such subtlety that they thought her mad. A woman never much more negotiable than William Blake' – whom her daughters loved with a fierce passion, and longed to protect, and had to resist. The mother, in other words, of fatherless daughters.

Now Mrs Fairfield takes the baby:

'I'm glad it's a boy,' she says to you. 'Boys have an easier life.'

And she sighs. This woman loved her faithless husband to distraction, perhaps as Amy/Jane loves Wells? Perhaps as women do love men who are kind to them when they remember them, but who mostly just forget? Masochism enters the female soul all too easily: like couch-grass into a garden, impossible to eradicate, twining deep beneath the soil, stifling other healthy, cheerful, ordinary growths.

Mother smiles; she suffers: she pats your hand. If she spoke her mind you know she'd say, 'So here you are, Rebecca! After all the years of sacrifice on my part, the struggle to make ends meet, to have you educated, so you could live a decent life independent of male whim – all you have done is throw it all away, and become the sexual and emotional plaything of a married man, old enough to be your father. In throwing your life away you have thrown away mine. You are all I have!' Which she doesn't say, and just as well, because it isn't true; because anyway actually she has Letty – her blonde and blue-eyed brilliant eldest, cool and tough and ambitious – and Winifred, wonderfully emotional and affectionate, and you'd like to remind her of that, and that you're not all she has, and beg her to be content with the two of them, and let you ruin your life in your own way.

'I expect he'll come and visit you soon,' says Mother next, and the words behind the words are plain. 'Why hasn't he been already; the profligate, the seducer, this man of many words and few acts? See where your worldly ambition has led you, Rebecca! This is what happens to girls who go too fast, who break the rules. Little by little, step by step, that's the proper way. Life should be nibbled at, not taken in the great greedy gulps you favour.'

The mere thinking of such thoughts, while holding the tongue, makes Mama's muscles tense: the thin neck swallow, the eyes protrude.

'Of course he will,' you say. 'Now don't worry and don't fuss!' You have already nursed your mother through a three-year illness. She developed exophthalmic goitre when you were sixteen. The sufferer in such an illness is over-active, agitated, emotional, subject to rages; the eyes pop, the flesh melts away. It is terrible to see the character and personality of even an acquaintance change with illness – it is almost unbearable to witness this in a mother. Near panic surges. Supposing she gets ill again and it's all your fault? The baby wakes, in response to your distress, and begins to cry. Mother soothes him, rocks him to rest. 'A boy,' she says. 'How I always wanted a boy.'

Well, we did our best for you, Mother! Don't speak it, Rebecca. Think it, but bite back the words. Wore heavy boots and kept our noses in schoolbooks and only ever went out to hand out leaflets for the Suffragists! But I couldn't ever quite do it, couldn't iron out my sex – though Letty's managing pretty well – here am I, in full female flight; leaking milk from my breasts, still swollen-bellied, all body, no mind, proving my point to you. Your fault, Mother! 'Well, now you have one as a grandchild,' is all you say, pacifically. Good girl!

You and your mother regain your composure. She holds your hand and pats it, and gives you the ordinary advice mothers of experience give to mothers of no experience, and all seems well. Then: 'I won't stay the night if you don't mind,' says Mother. 'I don't like the way the landlady looks at me. I suppose it's something in the end, that you changed your name. Now you can be Mrs West, quite reasonably, and the rest of us stay Fairfields. It's an ill wind. He really is a lovely baby, darling, and not in the least like his father.' 'I think he looks very like him,' you say defiantly. She smiles, the sweet, intelligent, indulgent smile she uses when you're talking nonsense and she forgives you.

'He'll marry you in the end, Cicily, of course he will,' she says. You would like to believe her, but how can you begin to explain the complexities of it all? You never really believed as a girl that anyone would *marry* you; you somehow never belonged to the ranks of girls to whom such ordinary, pleasant things as marriage happened. To marry was not to struggle, and all you ever knew was struggle. The effort of retaining dignity and composure in a world where, as far as you could see, you were despised by all around you, schoolfriends, neighbours, and all but a few teachers, for being poor, badly shod and *odd*. What price intellect, argument, books, music, art, the things of the mind, when the curtains are shabby and there's only bread and dripping for tea? Not even because you belong to the working classes and can't help being poor, but because Father's gambling it all away – when he's there – or has left you unprovided for – when he's not there – and the neighbours notice these things, don't think they don't. Duns, bailiffs and outraged

husbands – he's a philanderer, too – knock at the door day
and night, and Mother's eyes pop more and more, and the
more they pop the plainer she is and the more faithless he'll
be – and all your life is a series of humiliations: so you learn
how to dissimulate, how to smile, how, above all, to pass
exams. You become accustomed early to the knocks and
blows of life: you have learned how to accept them in the
solar plexus, keeping the smile on your face, playing for
time. Nobody knows you *care*.

You love your mother profoundly: you loved your father
with a passion. But how can you love your mother without
hating your father? It is a problem which can never be
solved, since one or the other was wronged so deeply. But
which one? The mind circles forever, like those revolving
discs of light on the dance-hall ceiling, changing from acid
green, to red, to blue, to violent yellow – into trust and out
again, into love and on to blame; feelings of omnipotence
changing on the instant to self-doubt, flickering into one
extreme emotion, out of the other, helplessly – until one
final night death pulls the switch and the wild internal
dancers are plunged into darkness. It's how, I suspect,
writers are made. The self becomes layered in youth in the
interests of survival: the layers can then be probed for ever,
the mind touching sore places as a tongue insists on search-
ing out a loose tooth, pushing and levering to see just how
loose it is, just how much it hurts. Sister Letty survived
another way: she glazed herself over in a brittle burnt-sugar
coat; poor Winnie couldn't cope: she trembled and suffered
from nerves all her life. While you, who learned dissimu-
lation, the art of not admitting defeat – a Saint Sebastian

who has discovered how to lift his head and smile though a thousand arrows pierce – you simply know that you must love the dawning day or else it'll be the death of you, and love your mother come what may. Stay cool now for your mother's sake, to stop her eyes from popping.

'Don't worry, Mama,' you say. 'It's going to be all right. The world is changing. People are not as easily shocked as they were.'

'I see no evidence of that whatsoever. Because you want things to be so, doesn't mean they are so. Cicily, what I cannot understand – why Hunstanton?'

'Why not Hunstanton?' you murmur. 'It's a perfectly pretty place. Mama, it was almost Llandudno. Think yourself lucky!'

And indeed it was almost Llandudno – when you were first pregnant Wells's plan was for the pair of you to take a house at an even more discreet distance from scandal-mongers, in Llandudno, in Wales. Wells wrote from Russia, where he was investigating the pre-revolutionary scene, that you and he could rent a house there and live as Mr and Mrs West – though he, being in the cinematograph business, would be away quite a lot. And there by the sea you and he would settle down and work and love – and you, Rebecca, would take care of him and feed him and keep him peaceful and comfortable. Dear God, Rebecca, didn't it occur to you – or is this obvious reaction confined to later, more sensitive generations? – that what your lover wants is a nanny, not a lover? And that it is simply not in your temperament to be a nanny! But of course, too late – too late, as always – you're pregnant – be grateful that you have the letters, those love letters, however full of fantasy they may be.

For of course it has to be fantasy – what was supposed to be happening to Amy/Jane and her two sons while your lover settled down with you in a Welsh seaside town? They couldn't just vanish. And what would happen to the World State? It was Wells's duty to keep that particular concept going: what would the Fabians say if he faltered? And how would the sands of Llandudno take such Wellsian poetic heart beatings as

> I am a Male
> I am a Male
> I am a MALE
> I have got Great Britain Pregnant
> She's greater than ever –

Wouldn't the same sands somehow swallow the lines up and deaden them and give back nothing, and depress him? Of course. And so the dream of Llandudno faded. The nursery that was the house that Amy/Jane built lured him back: Amy/Jane was Head Nanny, always would be. Naughty boy! Night-time cocoa and rompings on the hearth would soon make him better, and you, Rebecca, the flighty nursemaid, would be sent packing, back to the village, for carrying on with the young master. Wells came back from Russia to Amy/Jane, not you.

But now you have his son. Surely this will make things different, better? You sigh.

'Poor Cicily, you are so unhappy,' says Mother.

You shouldn't have sighed. The more she insists you are unhappy the more you are determined to be happy.

'I am not in the least unhappy,' you say. 'I just felt a little pain. The baby is only four days old. It is quite natural to feel a little pain.'

'You will have to come back home to Hampstead to live,' says Mama. 'At least in London we'll be able to find you a proper nurse. This one is a very vulgar type and probably *suspects.*'

You are instantly happy: Mother wants you home. And then instantly embattled: if you are at home she will tell you what to do, she won't let you see Wells, and she'll make you unhappy by the simple process of having no conception of happiness herself. Home means defeat. Home means a return to disgrace. Once you lived with the disgrace of an absent father but now it is you who will bring humiliation on the household. For love of you, mother and sister will try not to show it, will try not to mind, but to understand, forgive and support – but they will suffer.

No. You can't go home.

'I love it here,' you say. 'I love this coast. It's been such a wonderful summer! And much safer than London, with the Kaiser planning an aerial bombardment.'

'An aerial bombardment? No one would do anything so wicked,' says Mrs Fairfield. 'Good heavens, not even the Germans are such barbarians! Women and children might be killed! It's your friend, Mr H. G. Wells, I'm afraid, who has to be blamed for all this war hysteria. What was that absurd book he wrote? *The World Set Free?* All that destruction raining down from the air? So much rubble and debris! Only a cramped, fearful and unhealthy mind could have such visions. Of course he is not a young man. Older men do become embittered, I know.'

Bite back your retort, Rebecca. It will do no good. Instead, take up Wells's *Dream of Armageddon*, which you have by your bedside, and read this passage to her:

No one living, you know, knew what war was: no one could imagine with all these new inventions, what horror war might bring . . . the flying war machines, only one of the endless contrivances that had been invented . . . All sorts of things that people were routing out and furbishing up: infernal things; silly things: things that had never been tried. Big engines, terrible explosives, great guns. You know the silly way of the ingenious sort of men who make these things: they turn them out as beavers build dams, and with no more sense of the rivers they're going to divert and the lands they're going to flood.

(I've improved his grammar. If you have any influence on him, Rebecca, please try to get him to *read things through* before submitting them to the publisher. Precision of language and punctuation is simply not Wells's strong point.)

'Words, words,' says your mother, perhaps just a little impressed in spite of herself. 'He has no idea of human nature, or what is important in the world,' and she strokes little Anthony's cheek and you know that you will wait for Wells for ever, if you have to; because however little he knows about the human heart, he knows everything about human behaviour: and if he wants to live in a nursery, with Nanny, and Nanny is you, so be it. And you'll be a better one than Amy/Jane any day. 'Wells is a prophet,' you say.

'He understands the human race well enough to forecast its future.'

'To prophesy that only a few square miles of London will be left standing is plainly absurd. All such notions do is terrify the population.'

'He is not talking about this war,' you say, 'which is only minor, but of a future war, the one which will have to happen if the whole crescendo of waste is to be stopped. We are busily using up all the oil on our planet, all the trees, all the metals –'

'Absurd,' Mother says, her voice rising. 'This world is unimaginably big; these things can never be used up. Your H.G. is as foolish about the future as he is about his own life: and if he says you are here in Hunstanton to save you from bombs, you are a fool to believe him. You are here to be kept secret from his wife, and from his colleagues in the Fabian Society, whose disapproval frightens him to death.'

'H.G. is frightened of no one,' you say.

Try not to be upset, Rebecca, it's bad for you. Your milk will turn sour and give poor Anthony the hiccoughs.

'He is certainly frightened of the Webbs,' says your mother, sharply and accurately. 'The fact is, H. G. Wells simply doesn't know how to behave. It's hardly surprising. He is the son of a servant, and I don't care what anyone says, breeding shows.'

Unfair, unfair! All this talk of breeding! Your shabby youth in Edinburgh was haunted by the spectre of your family's noble past. Poor you might have been but proud you were – the more the neighbours scorned you, the higher you held your heads. So you had only one servant (even Karl Marx, when poverty-stricken in London, his children hungry, his wife dying because he couldn't afford a doctor, could manage *one* servant) when your neighbours had four, and what's more, had live-in fathers, and high Scottish teas with ham and eggs and baps, while you made do with bread and dripping, but never mind all that – your grandparents belonged to the gentry: they had titles, honours; they were literate, cultured folk who had paintings on the walls and books on the shelves, and so did you!

As for Wells being the son of a servant! Mother's estimate. No democrat, she. Don't let it upset you, Rebecca. Wells has earned his reprieve: he stands now above such class judgements. He talks to prime ministers, walks with kings, chides bishops and chats to revolutionaries. But I think you must accept that Wells is frightened of the Webbs. And there may be a grain of truth in what Mother says about that – would a *gentleman* be frightened? Would a *gentleman* be behaving to you like this now? Isn't it rather a servant's habit to hide you, his sin, away – as the butler might hide a silver spoon he's stolen? Is he not watering down your love with practicalities, as the cook waters down the sherry?

Rebecca, listen to me. The future's on your side, even if your mother isn't. Genes are all out of fashion now. The nurture/nature, environment/temperament argument has gone on all this century – sometimes swinging this way, sometimes that, but with the environmentalists winning hands down. If I say something (quite obvious to me) to the effect of 'writing runs in my family, it's in the genes', I am looked at oddly. That there might have been paper and pencil around and that this encouraged me, made writing possible, is accepted. That I might have been born to it, is not. Those to the right of the political scale like to believe in nature: it's to their advantage that they do; the left prefer to believe in nurture: it's a more hopeful concept. You can't change genes but you can change societies. That certain individuals are 'born to rule' by reason of their heredity is not an acceptable notion today. No, it must be access to power and the habit of privilege which enables the prince to step into the dead king's shoes and rule successfully. A mother who looks at her children and traces the family temperament here and there, back through the family tree, can now only be considered ignorant. Any good Marxist sociologist will say, 'What nonsense: these are learned characteristics, not inborn traits.' So you'd better believe it: don't rise to your mama's 'son of a servant' (and Anthony, by that reason, grandson of a servant) – bite back your reply. The future is on your side. You're in Hunstanton not because Wells is the son of a servant, but because he can get to Hunstanton easily either on the train from London or by motor from Glebe Place in Essex. So he says.

'You can't deny it,' persists your mother. 'He is frightened by the Webbs.'

'Not by the Webbs,' you say smartly, 'but by Webbery. By stodgy, fuddy-duddy reactionary ideas. Old Guardery.'

Your mother laughs. Her voice rises a little higher. 'Darling, that is absurd. The Webbs are socialists. Everyone knows. What happened was that your Mr Wells tried to take over their Fabian Society, most unfairly. He owed everything – all his important friends – to the Webbs. A gentleman would never have behaved like that.'

'Sidney and Beatrice Webb are quite mad and perfectly malicious,' you announce. But, Rebecca, you know that wasn't true. These two powerful and influential socialists were simply upset about Wells's scandalous affair with poor dear Amber Reeve, and so they should have been: she was, after all, the daughter of one of their Fabian colleagues. Wells was taking Free Love too far: he was bringing socialism into disrepute.

'He is frightened of them,' says your mother, acutely, 'because he knows he is in the wrong. To make that poor young girl pregnant and then disown her! And weren't the parents supposed to be his friends? That man has friends like no one else I know, in a manner no one else would dare. If he weren't famous there's not a decent household in the country would let him in the door.'

'Mother,' you say, 'you don't understand. How is the world to advance if women aren't freed from sexual inequality?'

Mother picks up Anthony, meaningfully, and rocks him and sighs.

'These things are important!' you persist. 'Here in the country we have to face our revolution. The world has to be freed from ignorance, injustice and illness. But it has to be done by consent, not force. Little by little, as the Fabians say. Like the Roman general Fabius, who won all his battles by advancing in just that way – little by little. And it's because it's all so important that quarrels arise.'

'At least poor dear Amber Reeve was able to get married,'

77

says your mother. 'I suppose sooner or later that particular scandal will be forgotten. But who's going to marry you?'

It is certainly unjust that, having brought you up to believe that you were not the marrying kind, your mother has now changed her tack and insists that you ought to be. But, as you will find yourself, later, one preaches all kinds of things to one's children, and then is quite appalled when they put them into practice: class equality, feminism, the pointlessness of passing exams, the non-importance of money. Your mother is only behaving like any other mother in making U-turns down some painfully busy street.

'If you ask me,' says your mother, 'marching under the banner of Free Love are a whole legion of devils. Lechery, treachery, greed, self-indulgence. I have every sympathy with the Webbs. What a come-uppance to Wells that the man Amber married happened to be a lawyer! And wasn't it Wells's idea that she married him in the first place? What a really stupid thing to suggest!'

'He had Amber's welfare in mind, Mama, not his own. And you know, she did chase after him shamefully. It was really no fault of his.'

You wish she would change the subject, but you don't want to suggest that she does. Talk of Amber makes you hurt inside, yet you despise the emotion of jealousy. You are indeed jealous and possessive, as what woman in love is not, and why indeed should she not be? If there is something of note and value here, surely it should be guarded! But you have put yourself in a difficult position – you have to pretend that you are not jealous, or what price Free Love now? And besides, Wells cannot put up with possessive women.

Amy/Jane isn't jealous, and so she's managed to stay his wife. It is, in Wells's eyes, her one great abiding virtue. No. You and he have to come together freely, joyously, unafraid, and so forth. Which means not nagging, complaining or reproaching, and *never* saying 'Where were you last night?'

'And what was all that about young Rosamund Bland?' goes on Mama, unstoppable. 'She can't have been more than sixteen at the time.'

'Rumour and gossip,' you say firmly, and good for you. 'Put about by base, limited, comic, timid and ugly spirits. There are so many people about who simply can't see joy, without seeing something nasty there as well.'

'There are so many people about,' says Mama darkly, 'who know all too much about Mr Wells. And how he seems to specialize in the daughters of his friends.'

That's more or less true. Rosamund is the child of Hubert Bland by one of his many mistresses, but brought up by the hapless Edith, of whom we have already spoken.

'Mama,' you say pointedly, 'at least no one can say *I* am the daughter of any friend of his.'

'Was I running him down?' asks Mama innocently. 'I'm sorry. I'm sure I don't mean to. I know how fond of him you are. I just don't see why you and he, if you think you have nothing to be ashamed of, spend so much time running here and there under false names, and practically putting on funny hats. Kiss Me Quick in Llandudno!'

'Scandal does no one any good,' you say, weakly.

'In other words,' says Mother triumphantly, 'Mr Wells is frightened of the Webbs. I don't see why you have to argue so.'

And she's won. Call Letty, Rebecca, before you start to cry or scream. And here indeed Letty comes, with a hot milk drink for you and tea for your mother, and just as well, because you have lost your moral hold on the conversation and are scraping the barrel of rebuttals.

'I'm trying to persuade Cicily to come back to Hampstead,' says Mama to Letty, brightly and unbelievably insincerely, 'but she says she loves Hunstanton.'

'She would do better to stay here,' says Letty, bluntly, 'until the fuss dies down.'

'Judging from today, the fuss will never die down,' you say gloomily, with more truth than you could possibly know.

Those who live (especially if in sin) with those whom the future will consider great, can't be expected to see into next week and behave with appropriate discretion. Those who are to be great themselves, as you are, can hardly be expected to trim their youthful follies the better to meet the future's backward glance.

'She's right,' says Letty, 'and it simply isn't fair on Winnie or me that she should come back home. We have to be more like other people if we're going to get on. And we were just beginning, at last, to seem to fit in – when this happens. I can put up with seeing Cicily's name in ridiculous maga-zines like the *Freewoman*; I'm sure I'm very glad she's doing so well as a journalist, even though I always thought she was going to be an actress – and put up with her histrionics on that account – and at least she uses a pseudonym so that people don't point to me in college and make remarks – but she's quite capable of asking that terrible man round so that everybody sees.'

'Letty,' says Mother, automatically, 'you mustn't speak to poor Cicily like that. You must think more of her and less of yourself.'

'All anyone has ever done since she was born is think of her! What about me?' Letty wails. And she actually begins to cry.

You must understand poor Letty, Rebecca. It is very hard, in your day, for a woman to get into medical school, or a legal college, for fear that the sight of a naked man or a naked emotion might coarsen her nature and make her unfit for motherhood and wifedom. (You see these difficulties as more or less normal: we see them as outrageous.) And Letty has done it! Now Letty has to be above moral reproach, not just for her sake but for the feminists' sake. And here you are, her sister, flailing and wailing emotion and protest, ankle-deep in Free Love, kicking up moral mud like a lawnmower on a too-wet lawn.

All three of you are weeping now. Anthony begins to wail. Nurse, eyebrows raised, takes him away to change him. Then you all embrace and begin to feel better.

Mother actually consents to take a cab back to the station, since it's raining so hard. Letty goes with her: she says she has missed too many lectures as it is. And you are left alone, with only Wells's folded letter under your pillow for reassurance, and these tenuous, probably hopeless, thought-waves from the future to comfort you.

You are tempted to shriek anger and outrage at Nurse when she brings Anthony back to you asleep and serene but sticky-mouthed again. Hold your tongue! Say nothing: don't offend her. Now's not the time. Count your blessings, and a sleeping baby is one of them. At least Nurse is not giving him laudanum. (Or we certainly hope not.) Sleep now. There's a good girl. Close your eyes.

And, Rebecca, if I can give you just one more piece of advice. Don't ask Wells, when he comes – which of course he will, very soon – to find you a new nurse. He'll only ask Amy/Jane, and I'm sorry, but I do think her 'quiet sense of humour', as Wells sees it, might somehow lead her to recommend one positively bound to cause trouble for you.

Safer to see to it yourself. Asleep? Good.

Dear Rebecca,

I wish you could answer me back. If only to say no, no, it wasn't like that: Mother said this, not that; you have Mrs Townshend's character all wrong; Letty *never* cried, that was the thing about her. Or even just to say, wearily, can't you please leave me alone. But nobody else does and, Rebecca, at least I'm on your side. Perhaps it's in your stars? Your fate to have your life and loves ceaselessly nibbled away at by posterity? Even by your contemporaries?

'Poor dear Rebecca,' said my grandmother, dissecting your nature, your character, your condition in the world. But it's bound to happen. The minute a writer puts pen to paper, raises the head out of the trench of anonymity, to look around at the war zone which is the world, and begins to report back, with excited incredulity, to those who safely shelter below – in whatever state of disheartening muddiness it may be – he or she gets peered at through sights from enemy lines, sniped at and shot at, and what is more, found fault with by his or her own side for not making a

better job of it all. Along with fame must go dishonour.
Writers are martyrs and there's an end to it.

In the meantime, concentrate on just how you're going
to escape from this room, this top-floor front of a Victorian
semi-detached in Hunstanton. Try and ask yourself whether
respectability and reputation are really worth this secrecy,
whether you shouldn't go and stay with Violet Hunt in
London and put up with the consequences. She's a gossipy
creature and loves events, and life there is at least full of
fun. I know what you will say to me. You will say, 'But H.G.
would never allow that!' Men, in your world, and indeed all
too often in ours, being creatures who 'allow' women to do
this or that. I know there is a kind of erotic pleasure in this
submission, this abdicating of the female will to the male,
but it shouldn't be encouraged. It leads to the supremacy of
male whim over female necessity. I hear it on the tops of
buses and in the supermarket queue – 'Oh, my husband
doesn't allow me to take the car on Sundays, to go out on
my own in the evenings, to have friends to lunch, to take a
job . . .' What manner of men can they be – these terrifying
law-makers? I meet them, and they seem, for the most part,
friendly and reasonable enough, not the tyrants their wives
have decided they will be. What you mean, Rebecca, is that
you would rather have the pleasure of doing what H.G.
wants, than doing what you want. And what he wants
from you is that you and the baby will exist when he wants
you to, not otherwise. And, as I keep insisting, that you will
never, never write any of those shattering novel reviews
again: which means not keeping the smart literary company
you need and love, but which he has no intention whatso-

ever of giving up. Therefore no Violet Hunt, no London –
just Hunstanton, Nurse and Mrs Crown . . .

Rebecca, here he comes! Wells has decided it is time for
you to exist. You hear his quick and slightly nasal voice –
he is in the house! – he is bounding up the stairs and Mrs
Crown is flattered and laughing and easy – and you haven't
even time to arrange your hair, because the door swings
open and he's here, a human teddy bear, rotund and mous-
tachioed, brilliant blue eyes beneath an absurd panama hat,
sweating slightly – and you haven't even time to wonder if
you really find him attractive, or only the *idea* of him attractive, because he has you in his arms.

'Clever, clever Panther! Oh, the mysteries! Oh, the
accomplishment! Panther, I love you as I have never loved
anyone! Do you love me? Say you do or I swear I will not
pay Mrs Crown a penny's rent and she will throw you and
the babe out on to the street.'

'I love you.'

'Again, again!'

'I love you, H.G.'

'What dark, grave eyes my Panther has. Did she suffer.
No, I can't have her suffer.'

'I suffered a little, but panthers are strong animals. Don't
you want to see the baby?'

And you call for Nurse, and Nurse comes and Wells does
not bother to disentangle his moustache from your hair and
Nurse raises her eyebrows before she leaves.

'She's a perfectly horrid woman and a bad nurse,' you
say, 'and feeds the baby syrup though I tell her not to.'

Wells doesn't reply: he really cannot hear domestic detail and talk of servant incompetence: he shuts his ears to it.

Now he hands the baby over to you, rather quickly. At least he hasn't tossed him up in the air and caught him, or worse, pretended not to be about to catch him, as some fathers are known to do, to the accompaniment of nervous laughs from female relatives and shrieks of equally nervous glee from the infant.

'I wish I could have come earlier,' says your lover, 'dear Panther, but I have to make the world a tidy place for this new man-child. And are you well, are you really well? Say you are, because it is a woman's chief duty to be healthy for her man's sake and her child's. And I will not have you anything but entirely dutiful.'

Rebecca, you should take him up on this point, you really should. Ask if it is a man's chief duty to be healthy, for his woman's sake and his child's, and see what he says: but you won't, you can't.

'I am very well,' you say. 'Soon I shall be writing again.'

'You must look after your dear brain,' he says. 'Rest it, just a little. Be content to be all womanly woman, a sweet unargumentative Panther, for just a little. Then go back to the young man's life! Put the baby down, Rebecca, so I can get my arms around you.'

You do. He tickles your cheek, feels your ear.

'Don't, don't,' you say, 'it's only a week.'

'Fear not,' he says, 'I am a moral pure quiet Jaguar, suitable for a position of trust.'

You wish you were more available to him. But you know what you've been told, and that's no. Abstinence, three months before the birth until three months after. What a penance life used to be!

'H.G.,' you say diffidently, 'now I have a baby it will be difficult for me to live a young man's life.' By which you mean free from sexual guilt and financially independent.

'I don't see,' he says, 'that that necessarily follows.'

'I have to settle down somewhere, you see, if I am to follow my occupation, if I am to earn. That means not just furnished rooms but a household. A household means a cook and a general maid. And some kind of female companion or else people will talk.'

'Do you care if they talk? Surely not!'

'Your wife might,' you say.

'Panther, Panther,' he says sorrowfully, 'your mother has been here, hasn't she, filling your head with silly nonsense, anxious worries. She should not do it! If I see her I will scold her. I will send her back to the chilly north where she belongs.'

'H.G.,' you say, 'don't change the subject.'

'Dear, dear,' he says, 'was I? My wise Panther, keeping bad Jaguar in order! What were you saying? A household? Does such a little baby as this have to lead to such serious, grown-up things? What, is my man-child to live among embroidered covers and crocheted tidies and gilded brackets and framed photographs and crossed fans and endless chatter about and servants, all the silly useless things that go with households?'

'Well –' you begin.

'Panther, our baby needs your warm bosom and a smile from your beautiful mouth and a healthy walk along the beach, not all those ridiculous *things*, and a loving father to visit him and a happy, free mother, unburdened by laundering antimacassars and the need for dusting framed chromo-lithographs of Jerusalem!'

Anthony begins to cry: he probably needs changing; it hardly seems the time to bring such matters up. H.G. is fascinated by the crying. 'What a rage he's in!' says H.G. 'Look at that crimson anger! I suppose all our lives are based upon rage.'

You wish he hadn't said that: what is he wishing upon your baby? Nurse comes in and takes Anthony away and the cries recede.

'In fact, it is the only explanation for human folly,' says Wells, 'that all our lives begin with rage. I expect he would rather be in your dear warmth, than out in the cold, cold world. I know what he feels.'

'I *can't* stay here, H.G.,' you say. 'In Hunstanton. What is Hunstanton to do with me, or me with Hunstanton?'

'But it's lovely here! The beach is wonderful!'

'There's no one to talk to.'

'There's me!'

'But you're not here all the time.'

He looks puzzled. 'I shall be here as often as I can. Isn't your Jaguar to your liking any more? Isn't he worth waiting for?'

'Of course he is,' you say, and he takes your hand, and smiles and says you have all the time in the world, and he has not because he is so old –

'Oh, but you're not,' you cry, 'you are the youngest, finest man in all the world –'

'And you are safe and cosy and away from the bombs here in Hunstar.ton,' says Wells, 'that is the main thing, and Jaguar will tell the folks back home in Easton Glebe he is wild for the book he means to write and must be away for a time, and the book he means to write is in Panther's heart, but they mustn't know that or it will hurt them.'

'What about the war?' you say, unmoved. 'Mustn't you be seeing to its running? Can that be left to its own devices?'

'The war! The war is all revelation,' he says, suddenly serious. 'It will change all our vision of life, of what can be. We are so paltry, despicable! Put us together, us human beings, and we become weak, timid, tiny, bad, angry. One man can be noble, two or more cannot. Any collective organization is worse than the sum of its parts –'

'Kropotkin made that observation,' you remark, 'fifty years ago.'

His blue eyes flash acknowledgement but he is not distracted. 'I was wrong to write of "the war to end war". I was in some kind of fever. Now the first casualty lists are coming in: instead of seeing that they are absurd, impossible, the nation is impressed. Supposing it goes on for years –'

'Surely not,' you say. 'People wouldn't be so mad. This war will, must, be over for Christmas!'

But he doesn't hear. He strides up and down: you feel you are a public meeting. 'The flaming actuality,' he declaims, 'is that the great powers are fighting each other in pursuance of their interests, after the accepted manner of history, and under the direction of their duly constituted military authorities, and there is nothing to choose between them. There is no room for the World State: it is crushed between juggernauts. We're fighting for King and Country and they're fighting for Kaiser and Fatherland and it's six of one and half a dozen of the other. Rebecca, in the last few days, while you have been lying here comfortable and cosy, my poor brain has been whirling and gasping! I am in a terrible state!'

How he paces about the room, all five foot six of him! Mind Incarnate, practically at the end of its tether.

He croaks, he wheezes, he speaks: 'Rebecca, it is almost impossible to grasp the imbecility, the violence, the moral feebleness of the human race, as revealed to us by the outbreak of this war.'

'What's to be done?' you ask presently, soothingly. 'There must be something.' He pauses, smiles, taking comfort from you. The world reels but love stays steady.

'I love you,' he says. 'You are so full of youth and courage. You don't understand despair. If there is something wrong, you still believe it can be mended.'

Well, the world does look much the same to you today as it did yesterday. That is to say, he is the most important person in it. You rock him and comfort him.

'Dearest Panther,' he says, 'you are the one light in my life: your woman's soul lifts me upwards, you infect me with courage; you are all womanly woman.'

'Really,' you inquire. 'Are you sure? When I was a girl and handing out Votes for Women leaflets, a little old woman brought her umbrella down with a thwack on my sister's head and said, "Thank God *I* am a womanly woman."'

That makes him laugh.

'All the same,' you say, 'you'd better not go round saying King and Country is claptrap, or they'll hang you for treason.'

'You can't hang Jaguars,' he says, feeling better. 'They're too slippery.'

He kisses you, and you kiss him and you're glad you have the baby, because that will join him to you for ever; and yet you know, because you are not stupid, that the baby will spoil things. Because however hard you try and keep it from him, babies must indeed have homes, and mothers who work must have nurses, and nurses must have their teas prepared by a cook, and soon you will be in the position of Amy/Jane: you will be a domestic person (he having done his best to make you one) and your lover will drift away in search of a less demanding, more exciting partner – the kind you were when the pair of you began. It is a phenomenon commonly enough observed: a man takes up with a woman who seems to be the opposite of his mother, turns her into his mother, and then deserts her for her opposite. Heaven protect the woman who encounters such a man. She will throw away her life, her identity, and be deserted for her pains.

And you really must consider this habit H.G. has of changing people's names, as if at best fictionalizing them, at worst depriving them of their past; starting them off, as it were, the day they met him. Jane – I call her Amy/Jane because she started life as Catherine Amy, commonly known as Amy, but Wells preferred Jane, so that was what she was henceforth called – was, Wells claimed, ready and willing to wear the name 'for everyday use and our common purposes'. Jane ordered a house well, according to her husband, and was 'an able shopper'. Well, just fine, forgive me if I go on calling her Amy/Jane in deference to that long departed, original personality. Would Amy have doled out the money for H.G.'s mistresses so calmly? Would Amy have paid so readily for a nursing home for a would-be suicide, yet another victim of her husband's search for the lover-shadow of his imagination? That 'aggregation of lovely and exciting thought: conceptions of encounter, reveries of sensuous delights and reciprocity' that he wrote about? Would Amy have paid the rent for Brig-y-don? Would she send you her own housekeeper to keep you and Anthony comfortable – as Jane is shortly to do? No. Amy couldn't. Jane, the alter ego, could, did. Poor Amy/Jane. Rebecca, I know you're too young to know what you're doing, but try and think what it is to be Amy, the mother of two, well into her forties, with a husband fancying so young, talented and beautiful a person as you. She must feel humiliated, hopeless, outclassed. Oh, what the hell! You won't listen. No one ever does. Did my grandfather's mistress listen to the voice of conscience? No. Of course not. Did your father's mistress listen, when your mother begged and pleaded? No. The trouble is, you're on Father's side, somewhere in your heart. So are all of us. These things are never done.

Well, never mind. At least you're Panther, glossy, sleek and young. You have a long life ahead of you, mate to his Jaguar. A rather elderly Jaguar, mind you, grey-haired around the nostrils, with perhaps already a spot of arthritis in the joints. And poor Amy/Jane will get cancer, as long-suffering wives so often seem to do, and die rather suddenly, fourteen years from now, and Wells will be overwhelmed, after her death, by a love for her he never particularly showed during her lifetime. She typed his work, though, very well. He always acknowledged and appreciated that, while she lived; and he wrote *a lot*, of course, and thus kept her properly occupied about his business, so although he may not have been physically with her, he was, she must have felt, in mind and spirit. It was only his body which wasn't there. Perhaps it doesn't matter so much.

'Rebecca,' he asks now, 'are you writing? I don't mean reviews, articles, general silliness. I mean a novel. You must begin soon.'

'What, here, now?' you ask, astonished.

'The nurse has the baby: the place is quiet, it is ideal.'

'H.G.,' you say, 'my body is in turmoil, my mind's in turmoil, the future terrifies me –'

'You? In turmoil? Never!'

'But I am!'

'What Panther needs is a wife. Panther needs sanity and care and courage and patience behind her.'

Now, Rebecca, hold your tongue! Do not say, intemperately, 'As you have Jane behind you, I suppose.' Enough to know he means it, that he is warning you. You do not make other people change the whole structure of their beliefs by complaining that those beliefs are unfair and inconvenient to you. There will only be a row. Smile, and kiss him. There! Well done.

'While I have you,' you say, 'while you are here with me, I feel better.'

'My spirit is always with you,' he says. 'And my feelings. You know that. So don't be frightened. Focus all these wayward emotions, to good purpose. Make the plan for the novel you mean to write.'

'A plan!' you cry, astounded. 'A novel should not have a *plan*. It grows, like a plant, like a tree. A nub of an idea: an acorn: you plant it, feed it, and suddenly it doesn't need you any more –'

'Rebecca!' he chides you. 'Be practical. A novel is a thing of reason: it is the means by which a writer correlates what he comprehends –'

It is what he believes, Rebecca. You are in different literary camps. Better accept it. Those in one camp give very little credit to those in the other. Crudely, you have this notion of art for art's sake: you believe, in an almost platonic sense, in Art, Beauty, Form, Literature – the novel which exists almost before it is written, an animation, a vision, taking not flesh but print. Wells sees the novel as a reforming agent: literature must, should, have a social purpose. The only excuse for fiction is that through it the world can be changed. If only there is enough information, Wells holds, there will be reformation.

It is too early in the world's history to tell which of you is right. Dickens, Tolstoy, Zola, Wells – those who write out of indignation, compassion, a sense of the fearfulness of physical existence – or those who are content to marvel at it, and rejoice in it, seeing sorrow rather than agony, beauty where others only see ugliness: Hardy, Henry James, Colette, yourself – you have no particular reforming zeal. You remain the property, the pleasure, of the educated classes. You are elitists, unpleasing to Marxists. There is too deep a division here, between yourself and Wells, for healing.

'What a bad and wilful Panther it sometimes is,' he says, 'for all its booful wild eyes. How will Panther bring a book to an end if it has no plan? It will go on forever. No reader will put up with it.'

'Panthers will just go on until they run out of steam,' you say, darkly, 'and readers will put up with what they have to.'

'Panthers are absurd,' he says. 'You must take readers more seriously. And what about my *Outline of History?* Is that supposed to manage without a plan?'

'You're not still meaning to write *that!*' you shriek at him.

In the next room Nurse wakes up: she and Anthony have been slumbering; he in his crib, she drooped over it. She thinks you are having a row. Well, so you are, but not of the kind she imagines.

'Of course I am,' he says, hurt. 'No one has written such a book before. It's what the world needs. We have exercises in national wishful thinking which pass as history, but no one yet has looked at the world as a whole, no one has pictured the developing communication of ideas, between nations.'

'I hate it,' you shriek. 'You are trying to put the world into a teaspoon and dose us with it, as if it were castor oil. You write such wonderful novels and here you are wasting your time –'

'Cold white sauce,' he interrupts. 'Old maid's view of sex – I know what you think of my novels – it's there in print for all the world to see.'

*

At which point he would usually fall upon you with erotic intent, because he knows – he has made certain – that you at least have no fault to find with his lovemaking: that he has your good opinion here! But today you are forbidden to him. The conversation, better ended here, continues:

'I was younger then,' you say, 'and ignorant. I had a virgin's view of sex.'

'You were hardly a virgin –'

'As good as,' you say. 'Young men are all energy, no skill. They are deathly serious, there is no fun in it at all! But you, you are the best lover in the world!'

'Dear Lord,' he says, 'are you sure I have to be a good and virtuous Jaguar? Do the doctors insist?'

'They do,' you say.

'They are not just being old maids?' he inquires. 'We live in a world of old maids, Mrs Grundies, poor frightened wretches who will think of any excuse to forbid sex. Are you sure this particular doctors' talk is not the same?'

'H.G.,' you say, 'it is five days since I had a baby. I am, simply, sore.'

He sighs. You suspect he holds it against you. You are right. He cannot easily accept that the female body he wants is not always in a proper state to receive him. He feels it is done on purpose.

'An outline of history!' you murmur. Please don't, Re-becca: leave the subject. You will destroy him. He in his way will destroy you: for you will love him for ever, never finding another to walk in his shoes. It isn't his fault. If a life is lost for love it is lost before love strikes. Love can only harm the already wounded. He stood in your way: you chose him as the means of your destruction, an excuse for your unhappiness. Unhappiness runs like a scarlet thread in a white cloth back through the history of your family: your father's father, your mother's mother. Why should you be exempt? Learn to accept it, not struggle against it.

In the meantime, take heart! You have your life before you: try to perceive the gratifications of requited love as, simply, a bonus, sometimes available, sometimes not, but not in the least essential to a fulfilled and useful life. You have before you a whole wonderful loom, ready strung, waiting for the broad rich fabric of your work. And Wells has behind him what will later be reckoned to be the best of his work: those strange, unhappy books of the prophetic imagination – *The Time Machine*, *The War of the Worlds*, and *The Invisible Man*; those singular books which did so much to explain the working classes to their betters – *Kipps*, *Mr Polly*, *Love and Mr Lewisham*; and the robust and knowledgeable *Tono-Bungay*. But what of his future?

'An outline of history!' you say, not to be stopped. 'How can history ever be outlined? It is stuffed far too full of marvels. Not even your brain can contain history, H.G. You will never master the world by reason! Don't think you will.'

'I can try,' he says. 'I will!' And so he does.

But you have driven him into a corner. He loves and admires you: he must defy you. You are female, he is male. If you live by emotion, untidiness, organic growth and inconsistency, he will live by their opposites. I wish you had stayed quiet: now he will write *Ann Veronica* and *Mr Britling* and a score of others, non-fiction posing as fiction, novels

REBECCA WEST

that describe but do not invent; he will no longer put his trust in that lively irrational part of himself that inspired his early works. It could have been different. Perhaps it is as unreasonable to lament unwritten novels as it is to lament unborn babies. But I do. Both. Not your fault: no, of course not, that henceforth he was to write these novels, not those: any more than your love for him was his fault. He encountered you. He listened to you; he could have stayed deaf. He spoiled love in you: you spoiled writing in him. I reckon you're quits.

He is in a bad mood now: he is edgy and irritable. You match his mood with yours. Let Jane do the soothing and stroking: you're worth better things.

YOU [*shrieking*]: Outlines! How you do like little ordered neat things. Like Jane.

HIM [*his voice going higher, more nasal, meaner*]: Leave Jane out of this! You can't complain. You are in no position to complain. You present yourself as a free woman, don't you?

YOU [*hissing*]: But I can hardly be a free mother. This was not in our original bargain.

HIM [*controlling himself, tendering a peace offering*]: I will live with you as much as I can.

YOU [*refusing the peace offer*]: Who decides how much you can? You?

HIM [*ranting*]: Rebecca, you are unreasonable! Try and understand. There is so much to be done. I am in a hurry. We are in a race; it is reason against ignorance, wisdom against folly. This war has shown me that. We thought there was all the time in the world: there isn't. We thought things would get better, slowly. That progress was inevitable. Now, all I can see is mankind destroying itself. It has the will. Soon it will have the ability. Men of goodwill and intelligence must stand up and be counted.

YOU [*shrieking*]: So me and my baby are to suffer because you must save the world?

Rebecca, calm down. Put your mind back to an extraordinary passage Wells wrote in *Tono-Bungay*, the last of his great novels:

To my mind radio-activity is a real disease of matter. Moreover it is a contagious disease. It spreads. You bring these debased and crumbling atoms near others and those too presently catch the trick of swinging themselves out of coherent existence. It is in matter exactly what the decay of our old culture is in society, a loss of traditions and distinctions and assured reactions . . . I am haunted by a grotesque fancy of the ultimate eating away and dry-rotting and dispersal of all our world. So that while man still struggles and dreams, his very substance will change and crumble from beneath him . . .

Rebecca, you have here, pacing up and down your room, in a bad temper, a prophet and a genius. Please pay him proper respect.

YOU: I'm sorry. I'll try not to be unreasonable. It's just I can't stand being addressed as if I were a public meeting.

That's better!

[*He takes your hand, strokes your cheek.*]

HIM: There is a war on: Panthers and Jaguars must make sacrifices.

YOU [*tentative*]: If I came to London and stayed with Violet Hunt –

HIM [*firmly*]: That would not be a good idea. She's a very gossipy lady.

Actually, Rebecca, Wells had a brief affair with Violet a few years back. He and she explored together, as you and he did, the world of convenient little restaurants with private rooms upstairs, and the struggling lodging-houses which are only too happy to let rooms to intermittent occupants. But it wasn't serious. No. It finished because he met the American writer Dorothy Richardson, and had an affair with her, though he liked neither her writing nor her conversation – oh, Rebecca, love among the artists! Better you remain ignorant of all this. No doubt H.G. feels the same.

HIM: Besides, if you stay with Violet I'll keep running into Ford and he's such an impossible fellow.

YOU: But I would have some company, my dear.

HIM: You're better and safer here.

YOU: But I can't stay here for ever. What's to become of me? An unmarried mother, an illegitimate child?

[*Your spirit evaporates, your mood swings, you begin to weep. Wells is not good with weeping women.*]

HIM [*chiding*]: Good heavens, Rebecca, you are young and strong. You will manage. Your mother has been upsetting you. I can always tell. Your family has no pity for you. Your mother and your sister are cold-blooded creatures

and you are warm-blooded and they cannot stand it. You
shouldn't listen to them.

YOU: They love me. Someone has to!

HIM: I love you, Rebecca.

YOU: Then marry me!

HIM [*very cross indeed*]: I am married already. What do you
wish me to do? Murder Jane?

YOU [*too late*]: I'm sorry, H.G. I just felt weak for a moment. I
suppose you are going now? [*For Wells has his timepiece
out and is looking at it.*]

HIM: There is a train at 7.15. I had better get it. You need
rest, to be well and strong again.

YOU: But I thought you could stay the night and we could
have a jolly breakfast together.

HIM: I expect the baby cries.

YOU: At night, a little.

HIM: I must sleep, because I have to write. Without sleep I
am a very bad-tempered, incompetent Jaguar indeed! I
will write you a letter in the morning out of all the extra
sleep I have managed. Panther won't regret it!

YOU [*tearful*]: At least look at Anthony before you go.
[*He does. He lifts the baby out of the crib and brings him in
to you, and lays him on your breast.*]

HIM: My baby, my mate. Soul mate, Life Mate. You mustn't
fret, Rebecca. All will be well.

He stands for a moment and stares out to where the low
sun strikes over the sea. He turns back to you. His eyes are
brilliant, brilliant blue, as if they've picked up the colour of
sky, sea, space. You can believe he's in charge of the world.

'This war,' he says. 'How can people know so much, yet be so stupid? It is beyond me. Really, I think I am defeated. What price science now? Guns and war-machines, and death!'

YOU: If science can build, science can destroy. Why are you so surprised?

HIM: Things seem simple to you because you are so young.

   [*The eyes glitter with tears. He touches Anthony's cheek.*]

HIM: Here we have a triumph of energy, of love, of excitement. Even as war breaks out, my baby is born. All the same, nothing will ever be the same again.

You do not know whether he is talking about the war and his shattered hopes for mankind, or of you and him. Rebecca, it is probably both. It won't ever be the same for the world again, or indeed for you and him again. Mrs Townshend will write Wells a letter on your behalf and he will relent and move you to Quinbury, ten miles from where he and Jane live; but when he comes to visit, the servants and friends will get in his way, and he won't have patience with that, and he will move you here and move you there, and you will pick up the threads of your career, and learn to live without him.

Let him go. He needs to go home now to assess his future: to face the turning of the ways, to decide which path to take – back into his own imagination, or forward into politics, reason and the World State. He will choose the wrong path.

The thing is, Rebecca – but I have gone too far; I hear your furious voice echoing down the corridors of the years: *Who does she think she is?* How does she *dare?* And I reply, stubborn, sulky and unrepentant as a younger sister, The one who should have been born after you: the one your mother lost: the one you attributed total maleness to, and total charm, in the form of little Richard Quin, in *The Fountain Overflows*, the voice that won't be silenced. If the world goes on scratching and nibbling away at what went on between you and Wells, and will not let the pair of you rest in peace, it is for good reason.

The thing is, Rebecca, the struggle was not just between male and female, husband and wife, mother and daughter, sister and sister, principle and lack of it, the future of a flesh-and-blood baby, but between the sharp power of reason and the vaguer, drifting energies of the creative imagination. You – the woman – opened the door to your lover: of course you did: and so you should. But he, the lover, there because he was a writer, should not have stepped inside (married men and younger girls, and so forth). The evil that men do does not so much live after them as hang around to rot them while they live. Most men are silent: the processes of their corruption are not apparent. But Wells! Wells wrote and wrote – what he thought, what he felt: he was a wonderfully noisy man. He didn't know what happened: he was too close to it. We in the future, his readers, can. Man and writer welded. Wells cultivated self-deception at your expense. He could not bring himself to proper feeling, to passion and despair: he stepped sideways into ceaseless busyness and self-congratulation. It did his writing no good. You – the writer who opened the door – were younger and stronger than him. Stepping inside, he took on more than he knew. Nemesis looked out of your dark eyes and lured him on. Unfair! You suffered, and won. Not suffering, he was defeated. You lost love: he lost literature and his future.

Let him go now. He is not as young as he was, this great man to whom posterity owes so much. He is looking tired – there is no special comfort you can give him: your body must be your own for a little. He will write to you tomorrow, another love letter for you to fold and cherish. Be grateful. Smile.

'Goodbye, my Panther.'

'Goodbye, my Jaguar.'

He is gone. Get out of bed, try your legs: they are not as weak as you thought. Take up the baby, go in to Nurse, tell her calmly there must be no more syrup. Start on the long road back to self-determination, to London, life without Wells, freedom and the future. It will take years, but you'll do it.

SELECTED BIBLIOGRAPHY

Fiction

The Return of the Soldier. New York: The Century Co., 1918; London: Nisbet & Co., 1918. Reissued by Virago, 1980; Doubleday, 1982.

The Judge. London: Hutchinson & Co., 1922; New York: George H. Doran Company, 1922. Reissued by Virago, 1980; Doubleday, 1982.

Harriet Hume: A London Fantasy. London: Hutchinson & Co., 1929; Garden City, New York: Doubleday, Doran & Company, Inc., 1929. Reissued by Virago, 1980; Doubleday, 1982.

War Nurse: The True Story of a Woman Who Lived, Loved and Suffered on the Western Front. New York: Cosmopolitan Book Corporation, 1930. (Published anonymously.)

The Harsh Voice: Four Short Novels. London: Jonathan Cape, 1935; Garden City, New York: Doubleday, Doran & Company, Inc., 1935. Reissued by Virago, 1982.

The Thinking Reed. New York: The Viking Press, 1936; London: Hutchinson & Co., 1936. Reissued by Macmillan & Co., London, 1966; Pan, 1969; Virago, 1984.

The Fountain Overflows. New York: The Viking Press, 1956; London: Macmillan & Co., 1957; Pan, 1970. Reissued by Virago, 1984; Viking Penguin Inc., 1985.

The Birds Fall Down. London: Macmillan & Co., 1966; New York: The Viking Press, 1966.

This Real Night. London: Macmillan & Co., 1984; Virago, 1984; New York: Viking Penguin Inc., 1984.

Cousin Rosamund. London: Macmillan & Co., 1985.

REBECCA WEST

Non-Fiction

Henry James ('Writers of the Day Series', edited by Bertram Christian). London: Nisbet & Co., 1916; New York: Henry Holt and Company, 1916.

The Strange Necessity: Essays and Reviews. London: Jonathan Cape, 1928; Garden City, New York: Doubleday, Doran & Company, Inc., 1928.

Ending in Earnest: A Literary Log. New York: Doubleday, Doran & Co. 1931. Reissued by Ayer Company, 1967.

St Augustine (a biography). London: Peter Davies Limited, 1933; New York: Appleton & Co., 1933. Reissued by Darby Books, 1979.

Black Lamb and Grey Falcon: A Journey through Yugoslavia. New York: The Viking Press, 1941; London: Macmillan & Co., 1942, 1968. Reissued by Penguin Books, 1982.

The Meaning of Treason. New York: The Viking Press, 1947; London: Macmillan & Co., 1949. *The Meaning of Treason,* 2nd ed. London: Macmillan & Co., 1952.

The New Meaning of Treason. New York: The Viking Press, 1964; (with title, *The Meaning of Treason, revised edition*) London: Macmillan & Co., 1965. Reissued, with new preface, by Virago, 1982.

The Young Rebecca: Writings of Rebecca West 1911–1917, Jane Marcus (ed.). Virago, 1983.

A Train of Powder. New York: The Viking Press, 1955; London: Macmillan & Co., 1955. Reissued by Virago, 1984.

The Court and the Castle: Some Treatments of a Recurrent Theme. New Haven: Yale University Press, 1957; London: Macmillan & Co., 1958.

Books on Rebecca West

Hutchinson, G. Evelyn. *A Preliminary List of the Writings of Rebecca West: 1912–1951*. New Haven: Yale University Press, 1957.

Olrich, Mary Margarita, Sister. *The Novels of Rebecca West: A Complex Unity*. PhD dissertation on microfilm, The University of Notre Dame, 1966.

Rubin, D. S. *The Recusant Myth in Modern Fiction*. PhD dissertation, University of Toronto, 1968.

Wolfe, Peter. *Rebecca West: Artist and Thinker* (Crosscurrents/ modern critiques). Carbondale, Illinois: Southern Illinois University Press, 1971.

Wolfer, Verena E. *Rebecca West: Kunsttheorie und Romanschaffen*. Bern: Francke Verlag, 1972.

Ray, Gordon. *H. G. Wells and Rebecca West*, London: Macmillan, 1974.

Books on H. G. Wells

West, Anthony. *H. G. Wells: Aspects of a Life*. London: Hutchinson, 1984; Penguin Books, 1985.

Wells, H. G. *H. G. Wells in Love: Experiment in Autobiography*. Two volumes. London: Faber, 1984.

Other

Film: *The Return of the Soldier*. Released by Golden Communications, January 1983; video released by Guild Home Video Ltd, November 1983.

TV adaptation: *The Birds Fall Down*. BBC Classic Series, 1980.